House
Warming
Classic Decorating Advice
For Homemakers on a Budget

D1559277

House Warming

Classic Decorating Advice
For Homemakers on a Budget

For Katherine

Mary Frances Yancey

By Mary Frances Yancey

Illustrations by
Lynn Lennon Johnson

EAKIN PRESS ◆ Austin, Texas

*TO MY CHILDREN, FOSTER, MARTHA JANE, AND DAVID,
WHO ENCOURAGED ME TO WRITE THIS BOOK.*

FIRST EDITION

Copyright © 1999
By Mary Frances Yancey

Published in the United States of America
By Eakin Press
A Division of Sunbelt Media, Inc.
P.O. Drawer 90159 ◫ Austin, Texas 78709-0159
email: eakinpub@sig.net
⌨ website: www.eakinpress.com ⌨

2 3 4 5 6 7 8 9

ISBN 1-57168-279-1

Library of Congress Cataloging-in-Publication Data

Yancey, Mary Frances.
    House warming : classic decorating advice for homemakers on a
budget / Mary Frances Yancey; illustrations by Lynn Lennon Johnson.
        p.   cm.
    ISBN 1-57168-279-1
    1. Interior decoration handbooks, manuals, etc.   I. Title.
NK2115.Y36   1999
747'.1--dc21
                                                    99-29703
                                                        CIP

Contents

House Becomes Home   v
Furniture.   1
Entrances   5
Living Room   15
Dining Room.   27
Your Bedroom.   32
Kitchen   35
Guest Room   39
Color.   41
Windows   46
Tables   53
Stools   56
For Your Walls   61
Accessories   71
Pillows.   81
Flowers   83
Etcetera.   89
Decorating Rules.   96
Vacation Home   100
Retirement Home   107
Note to the Reader   111

House Becomes Home

This book is written for people young and old, rich and poor who feel as I do that it is most important to live in an attractive place. Your home can be one room, a small apartment, your first home, your bigger home, your vacation home, or your retirement home. Money does not necessarily make things beautiful, and you may feel that you are not talented in decorating. In this book I hope to suggest ways to take the place where you now live, the possessions you now have, and transform them into a home which you find beautiful and attractive. You want your home to be a place of harmony, order, good taste, and comfort. To create this does not require a big budget—only courage, thought, energy, and imagination.

Any room can be made to be beautiful. I want to repeat, it is not necessarily a matter of money but a matter of harmony and comfort and decorating to your taste and idea of beauty.

I am told that self-esteem and self-image are greatly improved when people feel their surroundings are something of which to be proud. Many times I have been told that a person dresses better, is better groomed, and is more willing to entertain when he feels pleased and proud of his home. I am writing this book because I believe I have learned some things, some rules of thumb, which have proven to be true. There are many choices and many ways to pull a room together. The great challenge for each of us in making where we live attractive is to take what we have and put it together to make a home. Some possessions are from our grandmother's attic, some from our college days, some from a husband's bachelor apartment, some are wedding presents, some are mistakes which we bought. Whatever you have, please have the courage and sense of fun to come along with me and let me show you some ways to effectively use that which you already have.

This approach to decorating, designed to give you comfort in your home and in your life, is timeless, not trendy; solidly balanced, not tricky. I hope you will find this to be a "how to" book, a guide book of good taste and charm for the non-decorator.

The first part of this book contains a little history, a few interesting facts about furniture, some trends in decorating and why they occur, and my own philosophy of decorating. My aim in putting this book together is to pass on some things in decorating that I know to be harmonious. If you are in your first apartment and need a starting point, or if the room which has just been finished in your home fails to achieve the comfort and welcoming look you had dreamed of, perhaps this book can be a compass. If you are a new bride in a strange town far from home, this book may be the family friend with whom you can share your past and envision your future. If you are a single young man trying to make your new apartment into "your place," read on. Think about what you read and take any ideas as they appeal to you and sound attractive. Before you know it, your home will become distinctly your own—fashioned to your own taste.

Most of us are allotted a certain amount of space in which to live. What we do with this space is to try to make it become our home. Before we begin to discuss the specifics, let us see what "home" really means.

Home is your shelter and your refuge both physically and psychologically. It can be a place created by you for your comfort, your privacy, and your personal idea of who you are. There is no other area of your life over which you have so much control. It sets the tone of your life and the lives of those with whom you share the space.

Most of our lives are hectic and we strive for speed and efficiency in living them. It is important that we create a home so that our space becomes a refuge and escape, a place of comfort and privacy where there is an atmosphere of creativity and peace. Home is more than a physical place; it is also a state of being. The word "home" brings together the meaning of house, of household, of dwelling, of refuge, of ownership and affection.

The history of the home includes the development of the ideas and practice of privacy, intimacy, domesticity, and most important of all, comfort.

Comfort, like everything else, has its own history. The Latin word from which it comes means "to strengthen, to console." In the Middle Ages "The Comforter" was the Holy Spirit. Only in the 18th century did comfortable begin to acquire a sense of physical well being and enjoyment. By the Victorian Age, the word came to describe a long woolen scarf to wrap around one's neck. When we speak today of a comforter, we refer to a down-filled covering for the top of our bed to use on a cold winter night.

There is more to the development of this word "comfort" than a transition from the spiritual to the material. Its change in meaning involves the development of the idea and the practice of privacy. In the Middle Ages comfort was rare and the practice of privacy absent. Everyone, including royalty and people of great wealth, met, talked, ate, drank, slept, and sometimes bathed in the same room. Let us skip through time from that point, when all this happened in the same room, to our present time, when both comfort and privacy are part of the requirements of our home.

What essentially and exactly is comfort? Among other meanings, the one I am most interested in pursuing is "something that gives ease." The pursuit and awareness of comfort and ease is a whole way of life. I have made notes below of some things which say to me what comfort is. Each of you will have your own list to add to this.

- Comfort is shelter from wind, rain, cold, and heat.
- Comfort is being warm enough and cool enough.
- Comfort is a good bed in which to rest and sleep—big, smooth, compliant as a cloud, firm as a rock.
- Comfort is good light so that you see well what you are doing. (It is miserable to try to distinguish black from navy blue in a poorly lit closet, or to cook the evening meal with only a single ceiling light.)
- Comfort is an empty shelf when you are looking for a place to store something.
- Comfort is the absence of dirt or clutter.
- Comfort is a room where the young can make unlimited noise.
- Comfort is a special relic from the past, something brought from your childhood home to remind you of your roots and of the continuity of life.
- Comfort is privacy.
- Comfort is a place with a pleasant smell.
- Comfort is having something light and soft to throw over you when you take a nap.

- Comfort is a good pillow to fit your back.
- Comfort is your own chair with good light and a convenient table beside it on which to put your book or cup of tea.

And after all this, comfort is home.

"Home at last" is a phrase often spoken but more often felt, when, after a tiring day, you open the door to your special retreat. It is the place where you are completely relaxed. Home tells you who you are and where you belong. Home is where you know your way in the dark. Home is the place of rest and renewal. Home is the place for nurturing a family. Home is the place which makes you feel comfort and well being. It should make you fit better into the world outside the home.

When you are "home sick" (an interesting concept) you are longing for a place where you feel the sense of unity, security, and comfort which helped form your roots and define your identity. You will want to make your home the best of the old and the new so that it will offer the inner balance we all seek. Anything you loved from your childhood home is carried with you in memory and it is a part of you.

There are many areas in our lives over which we seem to have little or no control, but you can control the space in which we live. In this space you can create any atmosphere you want. Be kind to your space. The way in which you handle your space is important. You can create a mood. You can teach taste. You can see what color delights you. You can express yourself and create your own personal style of beauty and charm. To me this is most challenging and exciting, and it does not take money to accomplish.

This book is written to try to show you how. It does not take a professional analyst or decorator to walk into your house and tell what kind of person you are. You project whatever image you choose clearly and precisely, so be careful of your space. This means handle it with care. Be sure it says what you want it to say. For those who use a decorator, be sure to carefully choose the words you select in describing the look and the feel that you want in your room or your home. I am not referring to a period of furniture, color, or style. I am talking about descriptive adjectives, such as dignified, timeless, warm, peaceful, cheerful, smart, stylish, trendy, modest, quiet, friendly, daring, suitable— whatever it is that makes you comfortable. You are choosing the kind of refuge you want to provide for yourself, your family, and your friends. You face the exciting and challenging task of creating the greatest beauty, comfort, and charm in which to live. This is real control over your space. It is a very thought-provoking, creative job using all the perception, instinct, and analysis that you can muster.

It is said that real maturity is understanding the law of cause and effect and being willing to take the responsibility for your actions. I assure you that any amount of time spent thinking about your surroundings will be given back to you threefold.

A few more words about space. Space speaks a language of ceiling heights, wall length, proportions, angles, and relationships between open and closed places. These are things to be aware of. I have often wondered why some people cannot seem to work at their desks but can work in the middle of the living room. And why children who have a special playroom all to themselves seem to prefer to build their blocks on the kitchen floor? The need for human companionship aside, space itself has attractions and distractions that cannot be denied. Each of us must work toward making our space become so harmonious with our taste and concept of beauty and comfort that we feel that this is where we belong. This is home.

Let us think about your personal style. There is no greater compliment than someone saying this room looks like you. So what shows personal style? Personal style shines the minute you enter a room which is filled with the spirit of the person who lives there. Personal style is not something you put on like makeup, nor is it something you inherit. It is the real you shining through. It is always growing, always changing, being fine-tuned, and learning from new ideas. So as you are growing and expanding your style, let your rooms come along with you and they will be alive and exciting and fresh and warm.

How do you decide what your personal style is—the real you? I honestly do not know, but I suspect it is done the same way you decide about your personal style in clothes. You know that the way you appear, the clothes you wear, and the way you wear them is the you which the public and your family see as you. Most of us select clothes which suit our lifestyle, but we are also conscious of their being comfortable to wear. Both of these areas, clothes and space furnishings, are consciously learned. We do this by studying, looking at magazines, looking at other people in their homes, and by developing a sense of what we like and projecting in our imagination if this look is something for us. We also learn about ourselves by trial-and-error, shopping, window shopping, looking at our friends' homes, and remembering things we liked in the home in which we grew up. Looking and really seeing is invaluable in this area. All of these things help focus our attention and develop our personal styles.

Furnishing and arranging is in reality a design for living. Improving the feeling of a room through its decoration is an immensely creative task. Turn on the music while you are arranging your room. Do not be afraid to try something different if in your imagination it seems pleasing. Let us consider some things which each of us can do to give a room a lift and not turn the budget upside down by spending a fortune. Use your creativity: look, study, copy some idea which appealed to you. Change is good for all of us, to give us a new feeling.

You will express your personal style when you do some of the following things: rearrange your furniture, add some accessories which have been hiding in a storage closet, polish eight or ten red apples and put them in a wooden salad bowl on your coffee table, change the fabric on your extra sofa pillows from a conservative fabric to a luscious flowered chintz or a handsome toile, put out some fresh potpourri, remove the old magazines and put out some new ones. Do not be afraid to have mellow things in a room, things that are not yet shabby but show a little wear. Visualize this room to be the best it can be in beauty, comfort, suitability, smell, feel, and sound. Take a little time each day for a practice exercise as a way of keeping the spirit in shape. Edith Wharton said, "In spite of illness, in spite even of the arch-enemy sorrow, one can remain alive long past the usual date of disintegration if one is unafraid of change, insatiable in intellectual curiosity, interested in big things, and happy in small ways." I believe this to be true.

Beauty is defined in the dictionary as "the quality that is present in a thing or a person, giving intense pleasure or deep satisfaction to the mind. It arises from sensory manifestations, as shape, color, sound, and so forth. From a meaningful design, a pattern, or from something else as personality in which high spiritual qualities are manifest." And a later definition of beauty is "something excellent of its kind." I suspect beauty is a spiritual quality, but many would disagree. At any rate, I know that it is important to live in a beautiful place. This, of course, will differ for each of us because each of us is unique and we see beauty in a different way. Each of us is trying to create a beautiful atmosphere so that in our home we feel peace, quiet, and something that is simpatico with our nature and the meaning and purpose of our lives.

Nothing in this book is meant for you to copy, but I hope you will get some ideas that you can and will carry out to suit your individual taste and way of life. I hope it will spark your creativity. Remember, man is the only being on the planet with the unique ability to create. Remember also, it is not budget that matters, but taste and suitability, which are two different approaches to the same thing. And, please, remember comfort. When you are guided by good taste, suitability to your way of life, and comfort in making your space a home, home becomes a place which gladdens the heart, a place of retreat, a place of personal flavor. Put your special chair near a sunny window, toss a wonderful child's quilt, favorite afghan or mohair throw over the back of it. Turn on the music. Put your cup of tea on the table beside you. Settle in to look out the window at the great sights of nature and enjoy the peace which you have created for yourself. Mark Hampton, the well-known decorator, understood that it is the promise of comfort that makes a room visually inviting. Your home can be very restorative.

Please come along. The next section of this book will help you find specific ways to create your own beautiful home.

Furniture

The dictionary defines furniture as "moveable articles, such as tables, chairs, bedsteads, desks, cabinets, etc., required for use or ornaments in a house or office, any space where people need to be comfortable." I think it is most interesting that the word for furniture in several foreign languages is "moveable."

From the furniture section in the *Encyclopedia Americana*, we learn that climate and belief in immortality are responsible for more being known about Egyptian furniture than that of other civilizations antedating the Christian era. The custom of placing furniture and kindred articles in tombs to accompany the dead on their journey into the unknown furnished examples of what was used in their palaces. The dry climate of the Nile Valley preserved those items.

The Egyptians were partial to decorative furniture. The pieces were frequently enhanced by inlays of ivory, mother-of-pearl, faïence, semi-precious stones, gold, and other metals. Their cabinetmakers used, if they did not originate, such detail as mortise-and-tendon joints, lathe turned parts, box stretchers, rush or leather chair seats, varnish and grease.

Among the furniture forms were side and arm chairs with carved and shaped legs frequently terminating in paw or hoof feet, low three-legged stools, folding seats with X-shaped legs, settees, tables with stretchers, and beds with leather lattice work to support mattress-like cushions. The woods were sycamore, cedar, acacia, olive wood, yew, and ebony. Most of these were probably obtained from other lands because of the scarcity of any trees other than palm in the Nile Valley.

The Egyptians were so much the outstanding furniture makers of the ancient world that their forms served as models for other civilizations, such as Assyrian, Babylonian, and Hebrew. No specimens of furniture of these imitators have survived. Their forms are known only from contemporary descriptions.

James Laver, curator of the Victoria and Albert Museum in London, pointed out in one of his books the close connection between architecture, furniture, fashion, and economics. In times of war, civil or economic unrest or other troubles, the fashion and trend in furniture is sofas and chairs with generous rolled arms, and large pillows for a person to sink into and feel secure. Fashion in these times lean toward generous amounts of material, lace collars, full sleeves, and the like—a more feminine look. By the same token, in times of peace and prosperity when all is calm, fashion in furniture turns to sleek, sharp, cold, clean design or so-called "modern furniture." Architecture and certainly women's clothes also follow this trend. Peaceful times bring short skirts, very high-heeled shoes, and shorter cut hair. Is it not interesting that furniture and decorating follow our emotions and fill a definite need?

Let us go from the above comments on the history of

furniture and consider where you go to buy furniture for your home. There are furniture stores, furniture sections in department stores, antique shops, second-hand stores, estate sales, and on down the line to flea markets and garage sales.

What is good value in a piece of furniture? It is good workmanship, good design, suitability, and if an antique, a well-preserved condition. The other part of good value is in your personal reaction: a piece of furniture speaks to you so that you must have it for your own. You have a feeling for its history, imagining where it has been and seeing clearly that you must have it for now and for your future. To be more specific, when you fall in love with a piece of furniture, it has value for you.

You also may be fortunate enough to inherit some pieces from your grandmother's attic. It may be that you fall heir to something which has sentimental value to you. You have longed for the little, sturdy table which occupied her back porch and you will love it in your kitchen. Such things may have little value as qualities described above, but great human value and sentiment. The table will warm your heart and your home.

A few words on refinishing furniture. This is a serious business. Whether it is a wonderful antique or a reproduction which has been poorly cared for, recovering the finish is tricky business. I suggest you try some kinder treatments where you do not remove the finish, just work on the surface. There is an excellent furniture soap that, when used according to the directions, can remove the dirt and grime. When the furniture is clean, you can more clearly see what the real situation is. I do not object to a slightly used or sun-faded appearance as opposed to a "store-bought" look. But there are often scratches and white circles on wood where water has been left standing. An old, much-used remedy for keeping scratches and white spots is the meat of a pecan. When cut across, it can be rubbed on scratches or white marks and the oil from the nut will gradually darken the finish. This can be repeated and you will see improvement.

When you go to the hardware store, you will find there are many choices of furniture wax and polish from which to choose. Paste wax is more difficult and more time and energy consuming, but it does give lasting and pleasing results. Lemon oil is one of the easiest choices. It works well and gives a pleasing aroma to a room.

The final word concerning refinishing furniture is that if you decide to have a piece completely refinished, find out from your favorite antique dealer whom they consider the very best refinisher in your area. Plan to spend a considerable sum of money. When it comes home to you, it will still have the patina of a beautiful heirloom. I like furniture which has a mellow look, and a good furniture refinisher can produce this look.

Take care of your possessions and they will last many generations.

Acquiring furniture for this home you are dreaming of requires using your head as well as your heart, and, of course, you will need to pay attention to budget. Keep in mind our key words: comfort, beauty, and suitability.

Entrances

What does the outside entrance area say about who lives here? The space around your front door (and perhaps your back door) should be given some thought and attention. In realtors' vernacular, it should have "drive-up appeal." To the passerby as well as the guest, this first glance gives an indication of the people or person who lives inside. Of course, you want it to be attractive and inviting. You want some way to make a person think or say, "I'd love to see inside that house. I just know it has real charm." Once again, how do we accomplish this? How do you spark the passerby with anticipation as to what is on the other side of the front door?

To do this, I think you should make the front doorway the center of the picture. The door can either be stained or painted. It is a matter of personal choice. You may find dark black-green, pale blue, Chinese red, or a color that is suitable for your house and will be an eye-catcher. Whatever finish you select, be sure the door is spotlessly clean, kept free of dust and dirt on the surface and raised panels.

It can be adorned with a beautiful knob or latch, a mail slot or a mailbox near the door casing, attractive house numbers, a door knocker, and perhaps below or beside it a foot scraper. You choose the material and style of these accessories. If they are brass, please keep them brightly polished. The person looking at the front of the house will know "somebody cares." If all this is "spic and span," little else is needed to complete the picture.

You may choose a pair of suitably sized planters for either side of the door or the edge of the stoop. These can house a topiary tree or a sculptured green shrub. For a less formal, structured look use ivy or Asiatic jasmine which, on occasions, can be dressed up with a pot of light green or purple kale from the farmer's market, or a pot of impatiens placed in the center.

If your taste or the architecture of your house does not harmonize with the symmetrical look, try dressing only one side of the door. Put a large basket on the hinge side of the front door so it will be out of the way of people going in or out. Fill this basket with pots of green and/or blooming plants. Your arrangement may be more interesting if you raise the pots in the center by setting them on bricks to provide a focal point. What seems appealing and charming to you will most likely have the same effect on those who pass by.

On the subject of decorating outside front doors, I must admit to my readers that I find door wreaths unattractive except at Christmas. Perhaps this prejudice comes partly from my not liking artificial flowers and greenery. The other factor which makes me feel that it is "fresh material or nothing" is the fact that I grew up in a small town where a wreath on a door (except at Christmas) meant only one thing—that there had been a death in the family—so to me it is not a welcome, happy sign.

Now let us see what we want to make happen when a guest or family opens the front door and enters your home. What a person sees and feels at this point has an enormous impact. The entrance hall is the introduction to you, the person who lives here, and to your home, and to the pleasures which lie ahead. Here your guest feels that you want him to come in. Because this room feels warm and inviting, your guest will feel welcome. This space is the buffer between the hustle and bustle of the noisy, busy outside world and the private world of your home. Your guest will want to linger and take in the charm of the room, but at the same time be drawn farther into the next room, suspecting that what he finds there will also be pleasing.

Now, how can we do this? How can we make this "first look" at your home intriguing? It is the very beginning. Is this a little like flirting? "Entrance" literally means to charm, and it is a taste of what is to come. It is the same word as *"en'trance,"* with the accent on a different syllable. So we need to take this space, which is the beginning of a relationship with your home, and make it warm, interesting, and uniquely you.

Dwellings normally have two ways to enter: a front door leading into an entrance hall or foyer, and a back door leading into a back hall or service porch, which is generally used by family and friends and should be given equal consideration. They are both introductions to your home.

The first image after you open the outside doors, front or back, is a real, telling reflection of the person who lives here. What catches your eye? A warm color, a beautiful mirror, a glance into an open door down the way, fascinating prints up the stairs, and at the back door some gardening books handy to the outside. All these things quickly catch your eye.

Now, let us see what we can do to and for this front entrance hall to make it attractive and suitable to your way of life. Perhaps we should treat this room like a person, maybe "the real you." It is said that rooms have a life of their own. They become more alive when they are occupied, but they can have personality when no one is there. This entrance wants to give you a welcome and also introduce you and give an indication of your own style. So we need to give it your own special touch. Perhaps here is a good place to show some of your background and your heritage. This can be done with a wonderful heirloom brought from a relative's attic or from your childhood home.

Come with me and let's enter your front door. You may be wearing a coat, a hat, perhaps carrying a package, maybe groceries, the mail, and you may still have your key in your hand. You need a place on which to put some of these things. Perhaps the room's first need is a surface on which to put these things temporarily so you can take off your coat.

Here you and your guest face the same problem—to take off your coat and put it somewhere. If you are fortunate enough to have a guest closet near this entrance hall, let's have a look. We can make this inside box of a room become an interesting spot. Normally I do not use a lot of wall covering in decorating, but this closet is a place where I think treating the wall is a great thing to do. It is a surprise to open the door to get a coat hanger and see something interesting. I have often papered the walls of the closet with the blueprints of this or some other house. Blueprints blue is a great color. Because they are line drawings, they do not jump out at you or make the space seem smaller. These plans are often found at garage sales or flea markets. There are many wallpaper designs which are attractive in a closet. You may want to consider putting a fabric, perhaps mattress ticking, on the wall. If you do not wish to cover the walls, do consider a good strong color painted on the wall—a sky blue, a grass green, or any color which will make opening the guest closet a pleasant experience.

Let me share some information about wallpaper which may be helpful to you in a general way. If you decide to paper the three walls of your coat closet, you probably should get a professional to figure the exact amount of wallpaper you need. Wallpaper is priced by the single roll, but it is usually packaged in double rolls. American wallpaper contains thirty-six square feet in each single roll. A European roll has twenty-nine square feet. Be sure to order enough rolls of wallpaper for your job, because if the shop needs to reorder for you, the dye-lot may not be the same. Most shops will refund your money on an unopened roll of wallpaper if you overbuy.

Now we can consider some pieces of furniture which

will help make our entrance hall "entrancing." Perhaps our first need, as we saw above, is a surface. I suggest a table or a medium height chest of drawers. Over this it would be pleasant and useful to hang a mirror. In its reflection a mirror adds a dimension of space and light to the room. Also it is most useful. Anyone coming or going will be pleased to have a glance at the mirror to be sure he or she is ready to come in or go out. Do not depend on a ceiling light to illuminate this area, unless the only thing you wish to see is the bridge of your nose. You can achieve good light that combines with good decorating in several ways: a pair of electrified wall sconces on either side of the mirror, a pair of candlestick type lamps (tall and thin) on either end of the table or chest. Or you can use a more important single lamp at one end of the table.

On this same piece of furniture a most useful addition is a handsome tray. It can be wooden, silver, china, pottery, papier-mâché, tole (or tin), or whatever pleases your eye. This is a most convenient place to put incoming and outgoing mail. Remember, in all these selections we have mentioned so far and throughout your home, you have an opportunity to show your personal taste and style. Think of some tray stuck away, unused, in your storage space that will be just right for the mail. You may think, as I do, that this is a good place to have a green plant. Most halls do not have outside light, so if you try a plant, you will have trouble keeping it green and healthy with no light. Artificial plants or flowers are not the same as real—so let's not.

Now that we have the table or chest in place, a lovely addition to the furniture of the entrance, if there is room, would be a bench or a settee. This is a good place for the guest to put her outside coat. A cushion on the seat is an excellent opportunity for color and patterns. Extra pillows on the bench can add color and warmth.

And now we need something of interest on the wall above the bench. Have you ever fallen in love with a piece of fabric but in thinking it over realize that it is too bold, too daring, too expensive to consider using in quantity as the theme of a room? This is the place to buy one repeat of this fabric. Most fabrics are fifty-four inches wide and the patterns repeat at from twenty-four inches to thirty-six inches. Get your picture framer to build a stretcher as you would for a canvas on which to paint. Staple the fabric around the stretcher on the back side. You will need a friend to help you because this is a two-person project. Hang it above the bench and you will find that it is a very handsome addition to the room. Or, if you have a really interesting quilt, this is a wonderful place to display it. To hang a fine quilt, please do not put a nail in it or in the walls. Stitch a piece of fabric such as unbleached domestic across the back of the top of the quilt. This should be the width of a metal curtain rod, the kind of rod that is solid metal and does not bend. It is about the diameter of a pencil. Slip the rod into this sleeve and your quilt will hang without sagging. Hang it rather high so that it comes down behind the bench. This can also be done with a pieced but unquilted top using the same stretcher method. It gives color and design. These are easy to find and very reasonable at garage sales, estate sales, or thrift shops. They come from the lady who never got around to quilting them or got bored with the idea.

We are now beginning to warm this hall and to say "welcome."

If your entrance hall contains your stairway, you have an architectural element which adds interest to any room. I like a series of pictures taking your eye up the stairs. These need to appear to be a series or group, one size, and framed alike. They could be botanical, architectural, ships, details of furniture, any kind of print that appeals to you and has some interest. The color of the mat of these prints can be an important choice. It can be subtle or it can be daring, and it is something that deserves some thought. If the important big hanging on the wall over the bench is colorful and dramatic, the mat color of the prints should be quiet and blend into the wall. If the large wall covering is quiet, the mat color and prints can be the drama.

Depending on space and the shape of your entrance, you may want to use a center table, round or square, placed directly under the light fixture. This makes a beautiful entrance and on it you can put your mail tray or it can be a special place for a lovely tureen or a bouquet of flowers when you are expecting guests. It is a mistake for me to say "when you are expecting guests." Your entrance hall, I hope, will always look as though you are welcoming guests, or, as important, welcoming yourself. There are many ways to make your entrance hall entrancing and say "Greetings, come in, welcome, someone special is here."

Let's take a look at your space and see which of the suggested pieces you will want to try in your entrance hall: a table, a chest, one chair or two, a bench, a settee or small sofa, an umbrella stand, a mirror on the wall, lamps, pillows, a tray, and maybe a bowl of green apples. If you go to your storage closet you may see something not being used which will be just right for your entrance and the feeling you are trying to create. Make it suitable to your way of life, make it interesting, make it warm and welcoming.

I hope you are feeling that we have taken your front entrance space and made it something with real personality, perhaps a little drama—most of all something you feel proud and happy about. So let's take a look at the space into which the back door opens. The back hall can be really friendly and inviting.

The requirements of the two entrances are the same: a

temporary place to put whatever you are bringing into the house, a place to hang a coat, hat, or jacket, a mirror for a fleeting glance. In the back entrance, the table can be smaller and more country, less formal. You may want to use

a painted wash stand. It can still have a small lamp on it. This may be the light which you leave burning when you are out in the evening. Where do you hang your hat, your dog leash, your gardening jacket? You may select a hall tree

which was designed for just this place. In earlier times the hall tree was part of the furniture used in the front entrance. You may want to put some interesting wooden pegs in the wall or some iron or brass hooks. I really like the idea of buying an old

mantle shelf which can be found at a second-hand store or

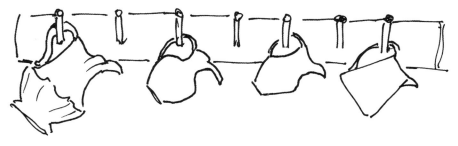

a junk shop and hanging it on the wall. The wood can be stripped and waxed, painted a heavenly blue, or left half wood showing through peeling paint. On the shelf you can put a favorite jar or pitcher, a watering can, a clock, some candlesticks. This is your chance for your personal taste to shine through. On the board under the mantle shelf, you can put six or eight hooks on which to hang keys, the dog leash, hats, and so on. This can make a unique, useful space-saving, convenient wall.

I hope some of these ideas will speak to you and will urge you to make your front and back entrances have such charm and interest that everyone will pause a moment and be "entranced."

Living Room

Let us discuss furniture and its placement one room at a time, beginning with the living room. Perhaps, although I hope not, your living room is misnamed and is seldom used. As a result it becomes cold, still, and unwelcoming. The time is now to change this room and make it become a "lived in" room which creates and radiates warmth, welcome and comfort, as well as beauty and suitability to your way of life.

Begin your work and study by going into this room and selecting the spot in which you would most like to sit if you were alone in the room. Stop and think how you could use this room on a daily basis.

Now let's see what it is that gives a room comfort and harmony. First is the proper placement and arrangement of furniture. This means good seating for you alone and/or for two, four, six or eight people who can all hear the conversation. To begin with, you need to find a focal point of your room, the center around which to build. If there is a fireplace, this is an obvious point of interest, and since a fireplace is not furniture, not moveable, and fixed in its location, it is the first choice as a focal point. The hearth, by definition, means "the heart of the home." If you do not have a fireplace, perhaps your room has a bay window or a large window with a view. If your room has neither of these, consider as the focal point:

(1)   a large table, dining or library size with something interesting hanging over it;
(2)   a secretary;
(3)   a desk or a chest of drawers also with something important hanging above it for height. It could be a group of prints, botanical, ships, architectural, or a large family portrait (if you are lucky enough to have one) or a hanging shelf. (More details on what to put on the hanging shelves in different rooms can be found in the chapter on wall decoration).

After you decide on the focal point of your room, begin to think of the proper arrangement of your furniture for the way you live in the space allotted to you. This room should be warm, clean, and uncluttered at this point, rather like an empty canvas on which you will paint a picture. It should smell fresh (and not as though you have recently sprayed the area with something to kill an unpleasant odor), the fresh smell coming from a flower or a bowl of potpourri. Pull a chair by the window and enjoy the sun while you are studying the room that is soon to become your home. Be creative with your space. The watchwords here are study, copy, and adapt your furniture to new uses, such as a small chest on which the top lifts to be used for a coffee table. This begins to bring your personal style into your rooms.

Do not forget to turn on music which lifts your spirits while you are daydreaming about your rooms. Get a good, patient friend to come for a few hours and help you move furniture (and be prepared to return the favor). Take one room at a time and make it the best you can make it. Make it "you" in beauty, comfort, smell, vision, and sound so that you enjoy and feel your spirits lifted every time you walk in.

Now we will go to the idea of placing furniture, building around your focal point, which does not move.

"Borrowing ideas is one of the time-honored approaches to decorating." Sister Parrish, the famous decorator, also often tells her fellow designers: "Original and creative decorating involves giving a room your own distinctive voice." There are really no problem rooms; there are simply some rooms that have difficult and unusual features which wait for you to use your own creative approach. Slow down, wait a minute or two, think a lot. Begin by analyzing your room—how to put the furniture together for the most comfort, how the light can set the mood, where you need a spot of color, where you need some height, where your favorite accessory will give the most impact. You are then beginning to get acquainted with your space and with yourself. Will it be comfortable for you? If so, the chances are that it will be welcoming and comforting to someone else.

In his writings about decorating rooms, Mark Hampton, the well-known decorator, emphasized the fine points of placement. The rooms that require a lot of study are so called "public rooms," rooms in which you live but also entertain others. This is a room in which conversation can flourish, whether between you and one other person or among eight people. This is a room where people feel at home, and comfortable, where people would rather sit than stand. This is a room which is well arranged, is gently pleasing to the eye, and provides physical comfort and warmth.

When you look at a room that attracts you, see if you can put your finger on what draws your attention. Is it the color? Is it the scale? Is it the focus? Or is it one particular corner or grouping of furniture which seems to draw you to it because of its warmth? Don't ever let your room become austere and too formal unless that is really your life-style and you have chosen it knowingly and with thought. In that case the chances are fairly good that you will never pick up this book for help and guidance. Remember that the focus of decorating is living comfortably in your space and making your room fit you and your needs. Remember beauty and comfort when you are placing your furniture. Where there is seating, always try to put a table nearby for lighting, a place to put your glass, your teacup, your sewing, or your book.

And now the question: Where to put the furniture? No room will look its best until it is comfortably arranged. What does this mean? It means stop, think, and conclude realistically what you are going to do in this living room. Most likely you, your family, and friends are the ones who will use and enjoy this living room. Arranging and planning a room for entertaining large groups is important because most people only do this a few times a year. You usually entertain only the number of people you can seat at your dining table, and this number seldom exceeds twelve. For comfortable sitting the chairs should have some variation in scale—some large, some small. Don't be afraid of stools and benches. Some of the chair seats should be firm and a little higher than the average reading chair. Many people do not care to lounge in low, squishy chairs; some may be afraid of falling asleep in them after a big dinner. Be careful in arranging your furniture so that you do not isolate a chair from the group. It will be the very place which the most shy, unsure guest will select and have a miserable, lonely time. As mentioned earlier, chairs and all seating require tables close by.

In arranging your furniture I want you to dare to be different and to express yourself, but I also want to make some suggestions which I hope you will find useful. Remember furniture means "moveable," so there are many, many ways to place furniture in a room.

When you are selecting pieces of furniture, I hope you will consider "versatility." For instance, a handsome chest of drawers is a fine investment because it is highly suitable and handsome for use in an entrance hall, dining room, living room, or bedroom. This is also true of all kinds of tables, and they are needed in every room. Many desks are versatile enough in style to go in several rooms. You may think of a sideboard or credenza as a dining room only piece. Try it in the master bedroom for a man to use to hold his "things." The height is excellent with a mirror hanging above. There are drawers to hold smaller items as well as cabinet doors for sweaters. On the floor underneath is an excellent place for baskets for extra storage or a straw Chinese suitcase. So when you are selecting pieces of furniture to buy, take into consideration the various places they may be needed and used while in your possession.

Let's spend a few minutes considering buying antiques. I am principally referring to wood pieces. None of the antiques I am talking about are of museum quality, but they should be dated well before the turn of the century (1900). The furniture should have a nice patina which only comes with age and, most of all, should be in a sturdy, solid, usable condition. First, you are helping our planet by recycling. In doing this you are saving a tree somewhere on Earth. Second, if a piece of furniture is more than fifty years old, you may be sure it contains no toxic chemicals. (However, if the piece of furniture is painted, it *may* have lead in the paint.) Third, very often an antique piece is less expensive than a similar reproduction. And should you change your desire to own it later, it is still an antique, but older, and not a piece of second-hand furniture. Fourth, do not buy anything just because it is an antique. Anything you buy should be sturdy and suitable for your style; you must love it and be barely able to live without it. Sometimes when you shop for new furniture, you may feel that the things offered you from your grandmother's attic have never looked so good! If a piece has questionable age (too little) but is just what you need and you think it fits what you are trying to accomplish in your home—and you can afford it—buy it. You won't regret it.

Most people have, want to own, or are acquiring a sofa as a basic piece of furniture. A rule of thumb for length of sofa is about seven feet. Even a very tall man can nap comfortably on this size sofa. If you insist on a longer sofa, please take note the next time you are in a group that the middle seat on the sofa is the last seat to be chosen. For some reason people feel trapped or hemmed in with a person on either side and often a coffee table in front of them. The stool or bench in the living room, even without a back against which to lean, is a more preferable choice. For comfort, if you can afford it, think about having some down and/or feathers for the cushions (both seat and back). I think spring and down construction is good for you to consider when you are buying. Down is less stiff, and more supple than a cotton-wrapped cushion. Down is the under plumage of a young bird, usually a duck. Pillows filled with down are delightfully soft and most luxurious. I prefer these above all else for comfort and a warm feeling. A word of caution: These pillows (for sofas, chairs, and bed) must be puffed, fluffed, and turned often.

What about the height of the back of the sofa? I prefer a back at least thirty inches high from the floor. A few inches here will give great comfort if you choose to lean your head back to rest.

There are many kinds of chairs from which to choose. Comfort, appearance, and scale will be your considerations. In general, living room chairs can be put in categories, such as lounge chairs, wing chairs, and pull-up armchairs. This gives you an opportunity to use your per-

sonal taste in choosing what is suitable for your comfort from what is available.

Where shall we place the furniture? Let's begin with the fireplace as the focal point of the living room.

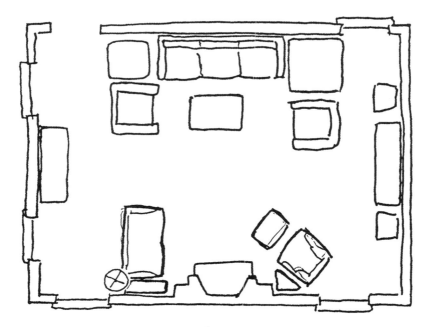

Plan A

Plan A. The most usual place for the sofa is on the wall opposite the fireplace. On either side of the sofa you should place a table (I like a generous size, maybe three feet) on which there will be a lamp. If the tables are smaller you should use standing lamps. This table height should be at least twenty-seven inches. At right angles to the sofa, beside each table, place a pair of lounge chairs, facing each other. To complete this group place a coffee table in front of the sofa. This area combines comfortable seating and good lighting with an easy place to put a glass or a cup of coffee for one, two, three, or four people.

For a second group, on one side of the fireplace and at right angles you could put a love seat with a table and lamp next to the wall. Opposite this you can place a wing chair, a smaller pull-up chair with arms, and a table between. In front of the fireplace, a stool large enough and high enough (seventeen inches) for seating a second four-person group. On any solid wall you may find an ideal place

Optional Plan A

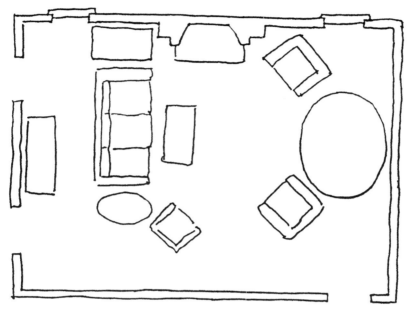

Plan B

for a large table with a chair on either side, a chest, a secretary, or a bookcase. Plan A is probably the most often
used arrangement, adapting for window and door openings of your particular room.

Plan B. Still using the fireplace as the focal point,
another possibility is placing the sofa at right angles to the
fireplace. Between the sofa and the wall put a table holding a lamp. At the other end of the sofa, repeat a table with
lamp or beside the table, facing the fireplace, put a chair
and a coffee table in front of the sofa. Opposite this group
next to the fireplace, put a wing chair or a lounge chair,
then the largest table you own, perhaps holding a pair of
lamps, interesting accessories, plenty of magazines and
books, and a comfortable chair at the other end of the
table. Once again put a stool in front of the fireplace, and
you have created a pleasant group for up to six people.

If neither of these plans is workable, see if your sofa can be centered on the longest solid wall in the room or centered on a window or a group of windows. The U-shape arrangement with a sofa and a pair of chairs at right angles makes a good start toward making your room comfortable.

A fireplace mantle, with something hanging over it such as a large painting, a smaller painting and a pair of sconces, or a group of prints, will give height to a room. On another wall try to get some height with a secretary, a chest with a hanging shelf over it, or a group of prints. You need different heights of furniture to add interest. Sofas, love seats, lounge chairs, and pull-up chairs are usually of similar heights. The addition of a wing chair and the pieces mentioned above will break the monotony of that one height. When I speak of a "pull-up" chair, I mean a chair similar to a dining-room armchair, which is easily moved. It may have an upholstered back and seat. This is often a chair made of bamboo or wicker. With generous seat and back cushions, this makes pleasant seating and is a visual relief from so many upholstered pieces.

Usually you should make an effort to balance the light in a room with the placement and number of lamps. I sug-

gest one at either end of the sofa, a lamp on a table or a standing lamp beside furniture, if your living room is on the large size or it is square in shape. A medium (forty-inch or larger) round table in the center of the room is very attractive. This plan makes two seating groups. You can add wing, lounge, pull-up, or straight chairs to this table, two facing one way and two the opposite way with the chair corner touching the table.

These guidelines may help you to determine the focal point in your living room and place furniture so that each time you walk in the room, you think, "I wish I had time to sit awhile in this place." Maybe soon you will make the time for this simple pleasure.

When you have completed the basic decoration of your room, try giving it a little test for comfort, suitability, warmth, and attractiveness or beauty. First walk in and look around. Choose a seat for yourself. What does the view from this seat say to you? Is it charming, pleasant, exciting? Any of these will give it a passing mark. Second, how does the chair, sofa, love seat sit? Too hard, too soft, too loungy, enough back support, do your feet touch the floor (too deep)? Comfort is the first test here. I cannot think of a seat which would be unsuitable for a living room. I can imagine a wicker or upholstered chaise in any except the most formal living room. The covering will make it suitable. By the same token, a formal sofa can be used in an informal country kitchen or bedroom with the right fabric. Third, does your chosen seat have a table nearby on which to put your things? Does your seat have good lighting, a table or standing lamp for reading or sewing? Will you enjoy going there for your second cup of coffee while you work the crossword puzzle? For comfort, warmth, and charm you may want to add a light throw (chenille or mohair is now so fashionable) over the back of the seat and, if suitable and there is room, an ottoman or footstool.

After you finish your test for quality, you may need to add something to the view. Perhaps the wall opposite your seat needs more prints or some sconces or a mirror. Is your chair just right for your sitting needs? As you settle in for a few stolen moments, do you long to spend the entire afternoon? If so, you've done well. If you need an extra small pillow for your back, remember this is a great place for a needed spot of color, or to show your needlepoint skills, a small tapestry piece from your travels, or from some forebearers' journeys. I'm going to guess that you have just the right thing.

If your seat fails to meet the comfort test, give it up when you can afford to—sell it, trade it, give it to the church bazaar—and replace it with a chair which gives you comfort. Everything in your house should furnish you with comfort. Work at it—little by little—until it does.

Dining Room

You may feel that your dining room needs to be the most formal room in your home, because it is used for ceremonial occasions—Christmas, Easter, birthdays, and family gatherings. I am always trying to bring warmth and a welcoming feeling into this room.

The dining table can be of any size, style, leg variation, stained wood or painted. And it's fun—and often preferable—to mix types of dining furniture rather than having a matched "suit" or "suite." Besides a dining table, you may want to consider six side-chairs (no arms) and a pair of upholstered chairs for the ends (very comfortable). These were very popular in the 1930s. They often have a small wing of three to four inches. Pay attention and be sure the arms of these two chairs slide under the table top. Or you may like the idea of two armchairs that do not match your side chairs but match each other. They could be painted or high-gloss lacquered to add some color.

When you select your table, be aware of seating space so that the legs of the table do not interfere with anyone sitting at the table. Also notice if the apron (the piece of wood between the top and the legs) gives room for a man's knees.

A side board, buffet, or credenza is a great addition to your dining room. The storage space is excellent for flat silver (in the drawer) and silver and china in the doors.

The top surface adds the warmth of wood, gives a place for setting out food for buffets and, between uses, is handsomely dressed with candlesticks on the end, and a soup tureen or china bowl in the center.

A second serving piece is also desirable, such as a me-

dium height chest of drawers, which is wonderful for holding your best table linen. On the top put anything decorative, or if you are fortunate enough to have a tea service,
this is a lovely place for it. I am most fond of a three-tiered
server, called a trolley because of its oversized brass rollers.
In the 1800s, a maid rolled the tea tray into the drawing
room or library. The less refined servers were used against
the walls of a hotel dining room and held pitchers of water,
butter tubs filled with crushed ice, and pats of butter, to be
handy for serving guests.

A plain console table from which to serve is also highly suitable for a wall. And a two- or three-tiered round table (also from the 1930s) in a window with blooming African violets or geraniums gives warmth and color to the room.

If you are in the habit of using your dining room only for dinner or for holiday dining, and if you need another reading and/or writing space, try moving your dining table at right angles to an empty wall or a window or (if you are lucky) into a bay window. Put two side chairs facing each other. If you have the space, put one armchair (the English call the chair a carver, for father who carves) at the end of the table, facing the window or the wall. Don't worry that some tall gentleman will now hit his head on the chandelier; go to the hardware store, buy an S-hook, take a tuck in the chandelier chain, and get it out of harm's way.

Now bring a table lamp and put it on the table, and you will have created a great place to write or read and look out a never used window. If you want to set this up as a work place for two people, have a pair of floor lamps on either side of the table. If you feel that it is harmful to the surface of your dining room table to work here, bring down your grandmother's quilt from your linen closet and use it to cover the table—for color, for protection, and for the pleasure of looking at the intricate patterns and stitches. If the size doesn't seem exactly right, keep turning it. Try letting the points (corners) hang down in the middle of each side. This is also a cozy look for warming a cold spot in winter. Once this dining room is put to this second use, it will no longer seem cold and unlived in.

Your Bedroom

Placing furniture and decorating your bedroom is very different from arranging your public rooms.

Your bedroom is your own very private and special space. This is a place where you can relax completely and retreat from the outside world. Decorate and arrange this room in whatever fashion pleases and makes you feel comfortable, luxurious, spoiled, and at home. Create a look which you love as well as one which makes you feel cozy and safe.

The following paragraphs will offer a few arrangements and placements of furniture to help you make your hideaway just the way you have dreamed it could be.

Usually a bedroom has one wall that is big enough for a king-sized or queen-sized bed. This big bed has become a most popular size in recent years and usually takes up a huge amount of space. If possible, try to find room for two large bedside tables so that all your needs, such as telephone, radio, good reading lamp and current reading material, will be within easy reach of your bed. At the foot of the bed try putting a big table to hold a TV on a lazy Susan swivel, with a lamp and a chair opposite the headboard to turn this into a writing table. An antique chest of drawers can hold your folded clothes (underwear, sweaters, and so forth). A mirror over this piece would look handsome and would add some height to the room, as well as quality and weight.

If there is a good window, try putting a table in front of it with a comfortable chair on either side and a stool to be shared by the two chairs. If you don't want to spoil your view out this window with a lamp, try putting a swing-arm lamp on the wall of the casing of each side of the window or a standing light, and make sure they are all good reading lights. At the foot of the bed, if you do not like the table idea, try a love seat, a sofa, or a wooden bench. Another useful possibility would be a low chest the size of a small cedar chest with a lift top. On this you could have a boxed-cushion covered with your sheet or bedspread material.

This is your hideaway, your most special room, so allow

it to express your personal style. Be sure it has a good bed, adequate storage, a comfortable seating area, a well-lighted place for reading, and something handsome and most pleasing to you to look at opposite your bed as you wake up.

I want to speak a minute about adding an airy, less heavy look to your bedroom if it seems to weigh you down. If you own a bedstead with a headboard and a footboard and finished side rails, consider leaving the underpart open. To do this you need to upholster the bedsprings. Actually, you can put a fitted sheet on the springs so that no metal springs or ticking show. Then for a spread, buy a coverlet that hangs down over part of the springs. The open look under the bed is a relief from the heavy draperied look of a bedspread that comes to the floor or a coverlet with a bed skirt underneath. This is a great new look with an iron bed or in a man's bedroom, and it is very, very easy to handle.

Kitchen

Kitchens have always been the heart of the home. In our pioneer history they served as the living room, and often as a bedroom, too, with a bed in the corner. Here is where people lived when they were not outdoors.

The popular country kitchen of the modern home has added to the basic functions of preparing food and storing dishes a comfortable sitting space, so that the cook is not physically isolated while preparing food for the family. The person cooking should be in the most hospitable gathering place for family and friends of any spot in the house. It is no wonder that at the present time so many dream of enlarging this space—taking in a back porch or breakfast room—to create a comfortable and welcoming country kitchen.

In the earliest kitchen the most important piece of furniture was a large, sturdy table used not only for eating but also for preparing food, writing, sewing, studying, and so on. Today you hear the expression "turn the table" used in many different ways which have nothing to do with a kitchen. This saying comes from pioneer days when space in the early all-purpose room was precious. The big kitchen table top at that time was not attached to its under-pinnings and both sides were used: one for cutting, food preparation, and rough treatment, and the second side, smooth and well polished, for eating and for company. Thus the expression "turn the table."

Today this big kitchen table is still the center of family living. A kitchen table of the best proportions which your space will permit is the first piece of furniture to add to your built-in counter, cupboards, and appliances. This table should be strong and sturdy. It will add warmth the minute you move it in and pull your chair up to it. Add a blooming geranium for the center or a pottery bowl of well-polished apples or lemons along with today's newspaper and you have a great place to start your day, or relax with a second cup of coffee, or welcome a neighbor who knocks at your back window or door. This table will be where you gear up for the day or unwind from it.

What kind of chairs should you have for your kitchen table? They can be whatever your heart desires and your pocketbook can afford. First, they must be suitable. In this instance, that means sturdy. Select a chair with good stretchers (the wooden pieces going between the four legs). This adds strength and keeps you from being nervous every time a heavy man tilts his chair on the back legs. It may be interesting to have several pairs of armless wooden chairs. You may add pairs as your needs grow. It's fun to search for them at flea markets, estate or garage sales, or in relatives' attics. For comfort and color make or buy a pad for the seat of each chair; the fabric will provide another place to show your individual taste.

Perhaps you can find room for a small table with a simple chair to use for your kitchen desk and telephone table. Try to situate it against a wall and put a hanging shelf above it to hold your cookbooks and your favorite pitcher. Underneath the shelf, put a wall lamp so that it will be easier to read recipes and make grocery lists.

If you have no room for the small table and hanging shelf, consider removing the doors from one of your cabinets, leaving open shelves. Maybe you can paint the back inside a bright color and use this as a decorative area. On the shelves place mostly things that you use—cookbooks, molds, pitchers, pottery bowls—then add a few decorative items, such as a small plant, a framed picture, and the like. This will make it feel like *your* kitchen, not just *the* kitchen.

What else can you do to warm and welcome your kitchen? Perhaps a small rug in front of your sink to add color and comfort and to make standing easier. Look around—do you possibly have room to squeeze in a wicker arm chair? See if you can find one of smaller scale to be made very comfortable with the addition of good, well-stuffed pillows covered in a pretty, colorful fabric for the back and seat. A piece of this fabric can be used for a small window valance or to cover a window shade or Roman shade. Be sure that the fabric hangs no lower than the window sill. The fabric can also be repeated in tie-on pad cushions for your table chairs.

These ideas will make your kitchen so inviting it will become a gathering place. Not only will the cook be happy, but so will everyone who crosses the threshold.

Guest Room

When furnishing your own guest room, think of the most welcoming, comfortable room (not counting your own bedroom) in which you have stayed away from your home. What were the things that made you want to stay longer?

Of course, the bed needs to be comfortable, with the nightstand or bigger table beside it. A good reading lamp is essential, should you have the leisure to read in bed. A comfortable chair in which to sit is an extra if you have room. Very often a guest room is smaller, so a table with a mirror over it can be used as a dressing table and a straight pull-up chair can double as a desk from which to send your postcards. There should be a hook on the back of the closet door for your robe and night clothes. You should also hang a fly-swatter and hook since there is nothing worse than a single fly, bee, or other kind of bug bothering you when you are just dozing off.

Other things I think of as necessities, not extras, are a box of tissues and extra roll of toilet tissue, a container holding safety pins, a needle and thread, and a small pair of scissors. On your closet shelf it is comforting to find an extra pillow and blanket neatly folded in case of a sudden temperature change. Be sure to put a glass in the bathroom. You will feel an extra welcome if you find a small bowl or basket of fresh fruit, a carafe holding water for drinking (in many vacation areas the tap water is not used for drinking), and a very small bouquet. You may think a large bouquet, but some people do not care to sleep in a small room with flowers giving even the most pleasant odor. If your guest has an allergy he can put a small vase of flowers on the closet shelf or in the bathroom.

Added pleasure can be provided by choosing magazines to suit the tastes and interests of your guests. Nothing makes you feel less wanted than a six-month-old news or fashion magazine, one with winter styles in the middle of summer. Two other necessities are a clock and a flashlight. A small plug-in night light is wonderful for the bathroom.

To be sure you have attended to the necessities and put some thought into your guests' comfort, move into your guest room and spend a night. Then you can take it from there and see what is needed.

Color

Color is everywhere, but it is important for you to find your part in the rainbow. What colors cheer you? What colors quiet your restless spirit? Color is powerful, and how it affects you deserves quite a little time and thought.

There is no color without light. Everyone is living in a field of color, never in a field of black and white. Many people have never given thought to what color does for them. Everyone needs to find a color palette with which to feel comfortable. Perhaps the first clue about you and color may come from looking into the closet where you keep your clothes. Is there a pattern in the colors you choose to wear? Some people are more cautious than others. You may see that you select a navy or gray suit over a stronger color or pattern. This does not mean that you wish to appear drab or conservative. When you selected this quiet style, you perhaps knew that a bright tie or a colorful paisley scarf would give it just the look you were seeking.

The same is true of a room. Remember that a few red poppies mixed with blue delphiniums and cornflowers can make any monotone room look charming and alive. We all rely on color to cheer us, to calm us, to welcome us, to comfort us in our very own place, our home.

Perhaps you will feel safer, more practical, and more comfortable in a neutral background of paint for the walls in your rooms. There are many, many tones of beige and cream and gray which do not jump out at you when you enter a room. These colors are subtle, quiet, and gentle. They seem to be "no color," but the minute you paint the wood trim and ceiling in the room white, you realize there is a contrast and a crispness and interest in this neutral palette. If you want less snap and want to be wrapped in quiet and peace, bring the wall and trim color closer together to show less contrast. I still prefer the ceiling a lighter tone or a pure white. Remember when choosing color from a small paint chip that color becomes more intense when used over a larger area like a wall.

A safe and practical way to select paint color for a room is to buy a small amount of your chosen color and paint it on a sample board at least two or three feet long. Do the same thing with the trim color on a smaller size board. When these two dry, you have an opportunity to move into various parts of the room—into a dark corner and along the wall opposite the windows where there is the most light. Here, where there is the most mass of color, the color will appear the strongest. Move the trim board along to decide how much contrast you like. Be sure to try these colors at night with overhead lighting and with lamps.

You need to feel comfortable in your choice of background. Comfort, again, should be considered suitable. Suitable really means appropriate good taste. When this is settled, you will begin to build your room. Perhaps you will find that you only want an accent of chrome yellow or delphinium blue such as can be supplied with a pillow or two, a bowl or cache-pot, a lamp, mats on a group of less colored framed prints. These things are easily changed and moved to a different part of your room. Fabric samples, a terry cloth towel, a scarf, a colored sheet, a piece of painted furniture are good things to use when playing with color.

I prefer living with a quiet but not dull background. I like accent color over which I have more control, both in deciding how strong and how much color I need. Look at the rooms where the walls are light and the wood trim is stronger and brighter in color. Now, if you feel you must have a place where a strong, striking color prevails, have courage but proceed on tiptoe. Paint the inside of a guest closet your favorite color, or if you dare a little more, paint your entrance hall a strong color and wallpaper the inside of your guest closet. What a happy surprise when you open that door and see beautiful flowers, a paisley, or a geometric design on the wall. A good two-toned stripe using the wall and trim color in your entrance would be beautiful. Let your creativity and imagination work in this space where you will not spend hours living.

Your back hall or entrance is also a great place to try a little variety and see how you like living with it. By boldly decorating these spaces where you do not spend much time, you will show a different side of your personality. Just passing through will lift your spirits.

If you want to make a real statement in a large space, consider your guest room. If you feel you have a particularly dark room, you may wish to make it appear lighter by making the floor light, adding something of sunshine yellow, whitewashing the walls, painting the mirror frame white, and so forth. Next in line after the guest room as a place to make a dramatic statement is the dining room. Forest green or some shade of red with sharp white wood trim are smashing choices. The dining room is used more often for the evening meal; it is not a room where one ordinarily spends hours during the day. Very often this room has a rheostat on the switch controlling the center chandelier. Candles are used for drama and make you feel like you are at a party. This is a place for you to be somewhat or very daring. What do you want this room to say? What is this room's principal use? If you are a young family with a small child and your dining room is your principal eating place, you need to choose a suitable color. Drama may have to be deferred until a later date.

Suitability makes a home work; it makes a home beautiful, welcoming, and comfortable. Think, think, think before you make a final decision.

Certainly you need the concept of a color scheme for your room. You need not have an excessive concern with matching all furniture in a room. Some contrast in color value is more helpful, and even a room aiming to be calm, restful, and quiet needs some drama. Different textures of fabric, as well as different tones of the same color, can add interest and make sure that you are not creating a color-deprived living space. A room of quiet colors makes a wonderful background for paintings and also for unusual accessories. Do not throw caution to the wind for major decisions, but for minor color options with a shorter life span make bold choices. If you love hot pink, first try it on a pillow or cocktail napkins for your next party or treat yourself to a gaudy hot pink amaryllis plant. Your craving for this color might wane in six months or a year, but you will have the pleasure of it while you love it.

There are may ways to improve your awareness of color and find your own part of the rainbow. Here are a few suggestions. For the next week, be on the lookout for ten colors that really catch your eye. It could be a snappy yellow sweatshirt, a hunter green car ahead of you in traffic, a basket of persimmons at the supermarket, a subtle blue to pink to mauve streak in the sky a minute after sunset. Write down what speaks to you. After a week look at your list. Try to recreate the colors in your sensual memory just as you recall a whiff of someone's perfume. Try to improve your awareness and memory of color.

Take a free lesson from the masters. Go to your local museum and stop when you are looking at a picture you really like. See if you can figure out what it is about the picture that attracts you. Select three paintings that you love while you are on the visit, and if possible buy a postcard of each and take them home with you. See what colors in these three postcards really attract you. Look around and see if you have any of these colors in your home.

We live in a world of color. How many shades of green do you count from your window as you look out? We seldom look carefully at colors around us. Color is to our sense of vision as music is to our sense of hearing and flavor to our sense of taste. When you become more aware of the beauty of these treats around you, you add another dimension to your life and your living.

All the beauty in our universe is here for us to enjoy. Make a beautiful creation out of everyday living and have a wonderful time. Create something new at home. You will grow in the creating, and so will your life. There is no limit to your capacity to create and to grow. Enjoy what you see when you walk into each room of your home and live in the comfort and beauty which you are creating. This is your world—dare to make and remake it in your own image.

Windows

How shall we treat the windows? Many books have been written on the subject of window coverings. In this chapter I will only attempt to suggest and guide you in your thinking so you can determine the why and the how of decorating your windows.

First the *why*. The purpose of covering windows usually includes shutting out sunlight and glare, providing privacy, and adding color and design at the particular location of the windows to give warmth and balance to the room. These appear to be the main considerations for a window treatment.

Now we reach the larger subject of *how*. Let us make categories of window coverings depending on the material used:

- Fabric will include draperies, curtains, roll-up shades of laminated fabric, Roman shades, plywood shutters covered with fabric.
- Wooden shutters, often with raised panels, include small Victorian louvered shutters or plantation shutters.

- Wooden or plastic venetian blinds.
- Under drapes—usually full length and made of sheer material hanging from a rod at the top of the window casing or a rod underneath the outer curtains. Brisbies are under curtains hung from a rod across the top mullion and ending at the window sill. These are most helpful where you have windows facing a public street. They afford privacy and light from the top row of panes.

Each of you will consider a *how* and a *why* which probably will be different from room to room. I advise you to

consider the outside view of the front of your house and see if the window treatment needs to be uniform for at least the first floor, a different treatment for the second or third floor, but still uniform.

It will be helpful to clarify some terms so that we use them correctly and understand what we are talking about.

Drapery is defined in the dictionary as heavy fabric used as a curtain. It is usually lined with a plain sateen fabric. *Drapery* is defined as fabric hung artistically at a window or a pair of doors.

Curtain is a term used for something hung from a rod which can be opened and closed. It often has pleats, hangs from a traverse rod, and usually is closed in the evening and opened in the morning. Often the fabric matches the

wallpaper in a room. Also, curtain and drapery fabric is often used for wall upholstery. All of these fabric panels can be effectively trimmed with braid, tassels, or border of a different fabric. All of these are areas of personal choice. You should look again and consider the purpose of these hangings from a decorative point of view and be sure it is the look which the room needs—privacy, light, and decorations (color or pattern).

One general word about the length of fabric hanging at windows. There are no general rules, only personal preferences and suitability to the room and its use. I do not care for fabric

draped out over the floor. My preference for length is about one or one and one-half inches above the floor so that when curtains are opened or closed they do not touch the floor. If the desired length is to end the fabric at the window sill, the fabric should barely escape touching the sill.

Let us talk a few moments about a *valance*, which is described in the dictionary as a piece of drapery hung across the top of a curtain. The purpose of using a valance is twofold: one is to cover a working traverse curtain rod or any plain rod, and the second is purely decorative. Your choices of size, shape, and material are many.

A valance can usually be made of fabric which is pleated or draped in the form of a swag hanging from a hidden rod. A valance may be made of wood which when painted or stained becomes an architectural element of the room. The wooden valance may be shaped in a decorative style or as a simple box. The

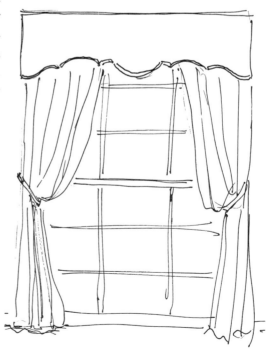

wooden valance is very often covered with fabric to match the curtains or draperies. Fringe, tassels, contrasting binding, cording, etc. are often used for the trim of the upholstered valance. Once again, here is an opportunity for you to use your personal taste and create your own look.

Let us turn our attention to non-fabric coverings. In American house history Indian shutters were an early necessity. Usually they rested on a deep window sill, were substantial in their thickness (usually one and a half inches), and were paneled and painted in a way to architecturally fit the room. They were strong enough to keep an arrow from entering the room. In the Victorian era, shutters of small divisions and small moveable slats were practical and popular. They gave privacy, controlled light, and had great versatility.

Later in our history, and principally in the Deep South, the shutters were of larger slats and gave more ventilation. These became known as plantation shutters. Plantation shutters are currently enjoying a great revival. They of course can be combined with draperies and curtains or can be used as the major window dressing. Shutters can be painted or stained to match the wood trim or to make a statement of contrast.

Mini-blinds and venetian blinds are all available in wood, metal, plastic and are an efficient way to achieve privacy and light control. There are many varieties from which to select.

Before we leave the subject of windows let us say a short word about *under drapes*. These are usually of a sheer material, hung from a rod at the top of a window and going to the floor or the window sill if hung inside the window casing. I prefer the rod to be a ceiling-mounted rod put within the window casing on the inside part of the top casing. The bottom of this curtain is at the sill.

On a job with a tight budget or one where a person has a rented space, I often use a very inexpensive material such as theatric gauze. This is wonderful material seventy-two inches wide, available in several colors: white, eggshell, brown, robin's egg blue. Moreover, the budget-minded cost is around three to five dollars a yard. There are two musts: double or triple the normal width for silhouette privacy (by which I mean a vague figure can be seen). The second must is a deep hem—the principle being the same as your having a deep (eight inch) hem in your childhood voile or organdy party dress. This is a smashing look for very little money.

Another under curtain treatment which is excellent for the need for day-time privacy is a Brisbie. This is hung with a spring rod or permanently installed brass or painted rod across the top mullion of the window pane. Brisbies can be made of any sheer fabric (my favorite is embroidered batiste). These are made with pinch pleats or a header, but I think no material should stand higher than the rod. This is my favorite style of under drapes.

General statements are dangerous, but I want to make one or two observations. Draperies usually wear longer than the same material used for upholstery. Do not be afraid to use different window treatment for windows in the same room. For a window seat in a room, you may find that a shutter is a good covering for the window.

Perhaps you will want a cushion covered in the curtain material of the other windows. I think shutters are sometimes troublesome in a bay window, if you like them open in the daytime. You might make draw curtains which pull from the center of the flat middle window and one panel on each of the side windows. Shutters could be used on the other windows in the same room.

Consider the *why* and the *how*. Bearing in mind that fabric is helpful in noise control, consider your budget, do not skimp on the fullness of the hanging panels, and make a selection which will be an added attraction to the charm of the room. Remember suitability.

Tables

Tables are my favorite pieces of furniture. I like big wooden surfaces. They immediately add warmth to a room. Every seating space should have access to a table. Nothing makes you more uncomfortable than wanting to put a glass down and having no suitable, safe place nearby.

Except for coffee and tea tables, I like normal table height tables, twenty-eight to twenty-nine inches for antique and thirty inches for new. With this height a twenty-four to twenty-six-inch-tall lamp is usually the proper height. If you are reading or sewing, this allows the light to shine on your lap where you need it, and not in your eyes. A nice wooden table top is a wonderful place on which to put your favorite things (see chapter on Accessories).

In your living room, space and common sense, as well as your personal taste, will determine the number and kinds of tables to be considered. I like a medium-sized table at either end of a sofa, each holding a lamp. The tables do not have to be a matching pair, but they should be approximately the same height (regular table height). The tables can be of different woods, painted different colors, or draped in a fabric. If there is room, I like a big table, perhaps between two upholstered chairs. This can be 3×5 feet or bigger if you have the space. It is a great place to put your personal touch: a group of books, a beautiful bowl, a green plant, and such, as well as a lamp or a pair of lamps.

In front of the sofa, I like a coffee table. This table should be the height of the platform of the sofa (where the seat cushions rest). A tea table in this location is also nice. It will be a bit taller than the coffee table but serve the same purpose. A finely upholstered stool with a tray on top of it is sometimes used in place of a coffee or tea table.

And now to the subject of dressing a dining room table. Set up the dining room table in the center of the room, under the chandelier. Everyone has his own idea of how a dining room table should look. Let me describe one arrangement I like. In the center place a living plant. My favorite is a maidenhair fern—it doesn't need any sunlight and if kept moist will last a long time. It is a beautiful, airy, light green in whatever container you like: a silver bowl, a ceramic pot holder, or a china or pottery soup tureen. On either side, I suggest a pair of candlesticks. If they are silver, they can stand alone. If they are china, glass, or pottery, they may look more finished standing in a hurricane shade. If the candlesticks do not appeal, I suggest a pair of pottery roosters (which probably need to stand at least eight or ten inches tall). Another thought would be four or six pottery egg cups planted with a couple of two-inch African violets from the dime or the grocery store.

In your bedroom, if you are fortunate enough to have the space, a big table on one side of the bed is a great luxury, and its use is obvious: a telephone, a radio, a good lamp, and whatever books and magazines your personal reading taste requires. Another great place for a large table in the bedroom is at the foot of your bed, perhaps holding a TV (run the electric cord from the head of the bed) and a good reading lamp for a comfortable chair placed nearby. If you do not have a big surface for your work desk, a large table in your bedroom is a must. Be sure to have a good lamp. To make adjustments for not having the usual drawer space a desk would have, stack attractively covered boxes and/or baskets to hold writing paper, etc. This is another good place to use interesting accessories: a special mug or short vase to hold your pens and pencils; a collection of open glass salt dishes for paper clips, thumb tacks, etc.; a handsome paper weight (an attractive addition) as well as a framed photograph or two; and, of course, a small vase of your choosing to keep a fresh flower.

A table, even a small one, is most useful in the kitchen for extra counter space, for after school snacks, or for enjoying a cup of coffee or tea with a friend. Often children do homework while a parent is preparing a meal. This table can be very attractive. I would buy an old wooden one at a garage or estate sale, paint it to please myself, and pick up chairs that are sturdy and easy to slide under the table. A simple jug lamp will be useful if the table is against a wall.

Stools

The stool is a wonderful armless, backless piece of furniture which comes in many shapes, sizes, and designs. It is interesting in decorating because it can be used in every room in the house, both public and private.

In the dictionary, *stool* is defined in many different ways —eighteen ways to be exact in the *Random House Dictionary*. The definition varies from the piece of furniture (which I think is the most common use of the word), to a term used in horticulture (meaning the stump, base, root of a plant), to a bird fastened to a pole and used as a decoy, a privy, a bishop's seat (considered symbolic of his authority), and even to the sacred chair of certain African priests. "To fall between two stools" is to fail through indecision to select either of two alternatives. In slang it means to serve as a "stool pigeon." It seems to have as many meanings in the English language as it has uses for us as a piece of furniture in our home.

The word *stool* began historically with the Latin word *scamnum* which the *American Heritage Dictionary* defines as

"a stool or bench serving as a seat, step, or support for the feet." An example: *scamillur*, "low stool," was borrowed by speakers of Old English as sceamol, stool, bench table.

In the chapter on Furniture, I speak about the important role the Egyptians had in the history of furniture. Our stool was among the pieces of furniture found when the ancient tombs were opened.

It has been stated that the Thebes stool may be the most copied stool in furniture history. The earliest known example dates back to Egypt's Eighteenth Dynasty (1567-1320 B.C.). At that time the stool was the seating of both king and commoner. This stool was named after the city of Thebes where many ancient treasures have been discovered. Since that early date adaptations and inter-pretations of the Thebes stool have been popular in home decorating and contin-ue to appear and reappear.

In our early American heritage, we smile with friendly humor at the use in Colonial times of the "duck-ing stool." This was used ear-lier in Europe and then in New England as a form of pun-ishment, consisting of a chair in which the offender was tied and ducked into water.

Today the stool serves many purposes because it can be used in different ways. It is hard to imagine the kitchen without a stool. You may remember one in your grand-mother's kitchen which when turned upside down became a three-step ladder. In a bedroom or in a dressing room, we find a normal-height stool of seventeen inches as a seat for the dressing table. In the living room, the stool can serve many purposes. In front of the fireplace, it completes the circle of conversation and if large enough can seat more than one person. Who doesn't love to sit and have the fire warm his back?

A stool is often used as a seat in front of a secretary. It is preferable to a chair, which might block the view of the beautiful intricate cubbyholes and small drawers so intriguingly filled with small interesting objects which do not wish to be hidden from view. A stool or bench is the normal seating for use at the piano. Most antique piano stools are pedestals with a round tufted cushion seat which can be raised or lowered to suit the person playing. More recently, piano benches seat two people because duets have been popular since the turn of the century. A relatively new

use for the stool is to place a large stool in front of a sofa that will accept a tray covering part of its top. This gives a firm place on which to put a glass, an ashtray, and some books. In other words, it becomes or replaces a coffee or tea table. For this use, it should be at least seventeen inches high from the floor and ample in size.

It is interesting that this backless seat finds so many places to be of use. Here is an excellent opportunity to introduce a different style to your room. Neither the fabric nor the wood need match anything.

One of the most commonly used kinds of stools is a low footstool. Footstools come in all sizes, shapes, and coverings. In earlier times stools were placed in front of each dining room chair, usually upholstered in carpet with two small ears for easy moving and no wood showing. They were designed so that each person could keep his feet off the floor and out of the draft. The houses were not as insulated and warm as they are today.

Other backless seats are ottomans, hafts, and hassocks, which are mostly intended for use in front of a chair for extended feet. We often see gout stools in antique shops. They, of course, were used to give comfort to someone suffering from gout by placing the foot against the bottom of the stool, situating the leg in the proper position to relieve pain in the joints. I think the shape of this stool is most attractive.

A stool is a great piece to add a spot of color and display a fabric different from anything else in the room. An upholstered stool provides a good place to use a more ornate or heavily carpeted piece because it will have a prominent position in your living room. A stool is a beautiful place to use a lovely piece of needlepoint. If a piece of needlepoint is too small or the wrong shape for the top of a stool, it can be mounted on a piece of fabric to make an interesting frame and to color coordinate with other fabrics in the room. Braid or a woven flat edging known as "gimp" can be placed to cover the seam where the needlepoint is attached to the larger piece of fabric.

Find yourself several interesting stools at an antique shop, a garage, yard or tag sale, and make them your own with your choice of fabric.

The moveable backless seat is a "many splendored thing," which will afford you an opportunity to show your personal style.

For Your Walls

Wall decorations are a most important element in room accessories. What you put on your walls varies greatly as to personal taste, suitability, lifestyle and your own idea of beauty. Some like more decoration and some like less. You may need to hang things lower in a dining room where you are usually viewing walls from a seated vantage. In other spaces, eye level from a standing view is the normal height of the center of a painting or a group.

A hanging shelf is a beautiful addition to a wall. Many of these hanging shelves were originally built to display plates. Each shelf had a groove toward the back and a strip of wood across the front to keep the plates from falling. These are most often seen in dining rooms and kitchens. They do not usually have a back in the shelf and the wall color shows through behind the plates. I often put a back in a hanging shelf and cover the back with bookbinding paper. Bookbinding paper, small in pattern and design, is used for end papers in leather books. It can be bought in sheets at art stores which supply book binding materials.

I really prefer the small all-over pattern in two colors, which gives interest and motion and shows a little between the objects on the shelves.

Hanging shelves can be used in any room where you need height, such as over a chest to give a room balance. I have one which I have used in several houses where I have lived, once in a living room over a three-drawer chest, and now in my present home in my dining room over the same chest.

What to put on the shelves?
- A small set of leather-bound books. If not leather-bound, books bound in a nice color.
- A suitably sized painting.
- An unusual coffee or tea pot.
- A piece of sculpture.

- A pair of urns, maybe even a silver one holding a little greenery.

   This is an excellent place for your special accessories and for your own style to show. Each accessory will be seen and enjoyed in this picture you have created. It is difficult to describe this in words, so please look carefully at the illustrations. If this is your thing, think of similar objects of interest you have tucked away that might bring out your own style. A hanging shelf is a great place for one-of-a-kind objects.

   In your kitchen or breakfast area, you may have room for a hanging shelf, probably a small, painted one, on which to put cookbooks, an interesting coffee pot or tea pot, and perhaps a copper or pottery mold. In the same field, you may find an antique mantle shelf on which you can put odd accessories or anything that interests you, and below it hang a good print or various molds. If this is in a hall near a back door, you may want to put some iron hooks underneath on which to hang umbrellas, jackets, or sweaters. If by chance you find a more formally carved mantle, you may want to hang it over a traditional sideboard in your dining room to hold three large platters, and perhaps between this and the top of the sideboard you may want to hang a row of plates or prints. Do not repeat the "three" number. Use either four plates or two large plates if you are using three platters.

   Hanging shelves can be found at antique shops, flea markets, estate sales, second-hand furniture stores, consignment shops, and garage sales. Be sure to measure the space where you plan to hang it. If the shelf you buy is longer than the chest or the table above which it hangs, you may want to put a pair of side chairs, one at either end. If there are chairs which do not go with other chairs, here is an opportunity for color and design on the seats. On

each side of the hanging shelf, you may want to put four or six framed prints or six plates to finish out this wall.

A single theme wall is an excellent place to show an owner's special hobby and interest. It is rather difficult to mix oil paintings, watercolors, and prints on one wall unless they have a common theme. When you do this, you need to be careful of the balance of the whole wall. Perhaps start in the center with an oil painting.

For example, in a man's apartment, fish could be a common subject. Put the largest and most important painting in the center. On either side, try four black and white or colored fish prints framed alike. Maybe you have a pair of plates with a fish design to hang outside the prints. If not, try adding a pair of brass, iron, or pewter sconces with some relatively short (eight-inch) candles. Beeswax candles are a good neutral color and do not drip. If you are a serious fisherman, you may want to frame some interesting

lures and hang in this group. You may even want to hang a wooden framed mirror as the center focal point if you do not have one strong central picture.

Another theme which is most effective is a sailing motif. It will work well if you center the wall with a sailing painting of some size and strength or an antique half

model framed behind glass. On either side on a wooden bracket you may want to add a sailboat, the kind used by children for a pond sailing. To finish the wall on the out-side hang four or six plates or framed prints which picture sailboats.

For the hunter, mounted animal heads and/or horns, mirrors whose frames are made from horns, sconces made from horns, are handsome and effective wall decorations. This decoration lends itself, as does a "fishing wall," to good conversation and tall tales which grow in the telling.

A theme wall is interesting, unique, and is easy to as-semble and hang.

Mirrors of all kinds are wonderful hanging on a wall. A small pair of wooden or gold-leaf framed mirrors can be helpful in a group on either side of a hanging shelf. The great thing about mirrors is that they reflect light as well as the interesting opposite side of the room. They are good additions to any space. You may want to take a dark, unin-teresting corner of a room and hang six or eight similar sized small mirrors down each side of the wall at right angles to each other. These probably could be as big as eight to ten inches, maybe twelve to fourteen depending on your room. They are easily picked up at garage sales.

A wall of plates formed from a set of six or eight dessert or salad-size plates which are interesting, colorful, and strong in design look wonderful on a dining room wall. These should be hung fairly close together, about two to four inches apart and in a geometrical pattern.

A pair of wooden wall brackets are great additions to a wall. They give that third dimension. In fact, I have done several walls of shore bird decoys on brackets using six or eight decoys. The brackets I find interesting are those that

are made of Victorian "under eave" brackets. On the top of these brackets you attach an appropriate-sized shelf to hold the objects. They are available in antique shops, flea markets, garage sales, almost anywhere. Currently, wooden architectural elements are being used to great effect. Because they are made for outside use, these brackets are usually of several different woods. I find it works better not to strip but to paint, sometimes antiquing them. This is a great accent and brings color and an opportunity for interest in a room. You can use a pair of brackets holding interesting vases, standing plates, ginger jars, figurines—whatever strikes your fancy—to put on either side of a big mirror to give width or height over a sofa or chest of drawers or anyplace you need something different on a wall.

I like antique quilts and also quilt tops as wall hangings. In the Entrance Hall chapter, I have given detailed directions on how to properly hang a quilt, so as not to ruin its value, and how to stretch a quilt top and/or a piece of fabric for hanging on a wall.

Long ago, pub signs, painted on both sides, were hung at right angles over the entrance to a shop or pub. These signs are enjoying popularity at this time as the enthusiasm for "Country English" continues. Also, antique fireboards, once used to cover empty fireboxes in summer, are wonderful hanging on the wall. These add an interesting touch in informal rooms, country kitchens, or vacation homes. The subject matter of both pub signs and fireboards will indicate to you their proper location in your home.

In putting up photographs, I suggest that you hang

them within a line border so that in looking at the wall, a person sees one big square or rectangle or diamond-shaped pattern of photographs. On the stairway, a group of prints, photographs, or paintings should be hung going up the walls with the same slant or angle as the risers to get the correct heights. The space between them really needs to be determined by the number of paintings in the group and how this group is seen both from the lower hall as well as from the upper hall.

Some people are very interested in old fabrics. If this appeals to you as something you would like to frame and do as a wall grouping, every flea market, garage sale, and most antique shops have a basket or a box full of old fabrics over in the corner. It is interesting to look for early crewel done by hand or machine, old toile which has patterns of dogs, birds, antique French country scenes, and ribbons and flowers and so forth. The fabrics are often off-white with the design in color—red, yellow, blue, purple, brown, and so on. Choose a frame, perhaps 12x16, of plain black without gold if possible, at any dime store and you can frame these yourself. Wrap the fabric around the cardboard piece that is in the frame. This is an inexpensive and effective way to show your personal taste, framed alike and hung as a group. I think you will find this easy to accomplish. It makes a good conversation piece and adds color and pattern to plain walls. If this group has four, six or eight pictures, hang them about three to four inches apart.

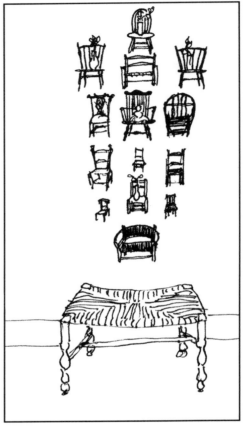

Recently, in decorating a young girl's apartment, I used a grouping of doll furniture chairs on the wall. These small chairs, all of a comparable size (eight to ten inches), were bigger than dollhouse furniture, some painted, some wicker, and some antique. They are hung visually as a group as if they are in a frame. They are constantly being added to, and everyone who goes on a trip brings her one. When this young lady has a party, she puts six or eight small vases like those you find in inexpensive import shops, each holding a flower, on the seat of several chairs. Individually, these chairs mean very little but together they are dynamite. Do you have something like this which could be made into a group?

Accessories

In fashion, architecture, and interior decorating, accessories play a key role in the finished product. These are the items which add the zip, the color, the accents, the interest, and personal style to a home. They reflect your taste and your heritage. Accessories are for every room. They are the dressing on a table.

In a recent column in *The Dallas Morning News* entitled "Whatever They Are, We Need Our Things," Ann Melvin wrote,

> My grandmother said it very simply, "I need to have my things about me." I have come to recognize that need as a political imperative of civilization. There is a sense of displacement that comes from not having one's "things"—a lamp, a pillow, the children's pictures on the bureau, a packet of letters in a drawer. *My things.*
>
> And as I walk through my home in the dark of night, comfortably navigating through my possessions, I smile to myself and admit that my need for things is not an aging condition but a human condition.

We humans do not merely mark our territory like a lion in the forest; no, we build monuments there, of new stuff and dreams and old stuff and memories and continuity, all welded together in a hodgepodge of relentless endeavor that at once identifies and elevates us. And if it gets bombed away or submerged or burned up, we will take the scraps and begin again, and if there are not scraps, we will invent them.

From the burned out and insured rich above Malibu to the bag lady pushing her grocery cart up the alley off of Main, to the old, the young, the displaced, from the ascetic in the rough robe and bare cross to the comfortable little woman wiping her matched set of teacups and hanging them in her cupboard, we all share a common resolve.

We need our things about us.

Ann Melvin stated that she has wondered what possessions people have in their parcels when fleeing flood and fire, but she did not discount them.

Books are the very best accessories. Coffee table books are a world of their own used singly or in a stack on any table. In choosing the books for the top of a stack, consider both subject matter and color of the cover. When you make your stack, it can be of two, four, six, eight, or ten books. I like the spine of the book turned toward most viewers. Coffee table books are good conversation starters when you are entertaining and having a mixed group of guests.

In another chapter, I suggested putting a set of books, a row of books bound in the same color (red, blue, green, or black) in a group of ten standing across the back of a table. This group gives stability to the back middle section of a table. Behind a tall, thin table lamp, a row of books such as these can be used in back of the lamp to span the distance between the table and the lampshade and are also highlighted by the light shining from the lamp. If you have a lamp that seems too short, raise it by putting it on three or four good-sized books (spines turned toward the room so the title and design can be seen).

Books are the finest things you can own to give a room a warm, lived-in look. A wall of books is wonderful insulation from cold, heat, and noise, and they are great decorations.

Let us talk about where to get your books. Probably you have brought some with you from home or school. Maybe you have some which came from your mother's or your grandmother's attic. Leather-bound books add great quality to a room. If you do not have books, please start acquiring them this very day. Reasonably priced books can be found at estate sales, tag sales, garage sales, and such. Watch the newspapers for used book sales at your neighborhood library. Five dollars often buys ten books. Old sets of books are very decorative, and often the print is too small to read easily. The material may be dated, but they are still fine for bookshelves or tables to use for decoration. Books have color, design, scale, weight, and can be placed wherever you need them, adding a great deal of quality to your decoration.

To arrange books on shelves, bring the edge or the spine of the books to the very front edge of the shelf. If books are too tall for your shelves, turn them on their sides and pull them to the front edge of the shelf. Incidentally, if some of your books are shabby but you need them to fill space, make a paper book cover out of a brown grocery sack turned inside out. Then, with black ink print the title on the spine, put six or eight similar-sized books together, and you have what appears to be a set. If you wish to put a group of books on a table and do not want to use outside bookends, buy a pair of simple metal right angle bookends like the ones the libraries use. Put them inside the cover of the end books so that they appear to be standing alone. This is very effective.

Coffee table books are just what the term implies—handsome, oversized, interesting to glance at—and they add interest to any room. You may want to take a child's chair, if you have one, and put it beside an adult's chair or in a corner with a large stack of books turned so that the titles can be read.

I very much like books in the dining room if you have a hanging shelf or a piece of furniture with shelves, such as a breakfront or a china cabinet. I think some books, particularly leather ones, are very handsome among china and silver objects. Even a small painting is a warming item. A big table in a room would look more interesting with a row of eight to ten books in a set across the back of it. More than money, an attractive living space takes time, thought, and effort. Your house should look like you, with your individual taste and your chosen accessories.

Boxes are excellent accessories. They too come in all sizes, material, and shapes. Everything you have is appropriate if you will pay attention to the scale in placing it. There is nothing more interesting than a good-sized, pretty box on a big table, maybe a three-by-five-foot table. It can be a closed box with a lid (hinged or free). It can be a rectangle, square, oval, or round. The box can be wooden, papier-mâché, woven, tin, lacquered, silver, covered with interesting paper, or whatever you have. Probably the most often used box in traditional decorating is a tea caddy, usually eight to ten inches or smaller. Many antique English wooden tea caddies are most interesting in their fittings. Often you find the inside divided into two sections, each with its wooden cover with a small ivory knob by which to lift it. In other caddies, a third division in the center contains a glass bowl which originally held a moist sponge to keep the tea fresh. A tea caddy often has the divider down the middle of the inside but no tops for the sections. In the days when much of our population smoked, these were filled with cigarettes for guests. Now we barely put out an ashtray, much less a cigarette. The tea caddie will give elegance, dignity, and quality to any table.

A box which I like to use, particularly in a man's apartment or on a big table or on a generously sized coffee table, is a tin box, almost always rectangular in size. These strongboxes originally protected valuable papers such as birth and marriage certificates, deeds to property, early surveys of property, and such. Strongboxes are painted high gloss black with a dull gold line for a trim and most often have the owner's name painted in gold paint on the end. Some of these were kept in safety deposit areas of banks or lawyers' offices. They have tight-fitting, hinged tops and often a key tied to the flat handle. I like to use these boxes very much. You will find them modestly priced in antique shops, at estate sales, flea markets, and so forth. They look wonderful and appropriate on a desk or writing table and are a great accessory for a man's apartment.

Oriental boxes add a different and pleasant note to your home. Presentation boxes may have long-since parted company with their contents, but alone they are ever so handsome. These boxes were made to hold a treasure such as a beautiful teapot being given as a gift. The box may be wooden, painted with lacquer (often black) with a terra cotta accent and a traditional design and border. Some teapot presentation boxes are made of woven straw with pewter latch hinges and a handle. If the inside is still with the box, it is usually of green velvet shaped like the teapot. These boxes are often found in antique shops, at estate sales, etc. You may see these particularly in cities in New England from which the clipper ships sailed to China with American cargo and a skipper bought a teapot to bring home as a gift for someone special. You can imagine the great stories that accompany a box like this, and it gives your home a different flavor.

Antique hat boxes are usually covered in hand-blocked wallpaper; often they are faded, delicate, and more difficult to find than the other boxes mentioned. Being made of a cardboard base, they are fairly fragile. One such box looks really wonderful on top of a secretary. It must be in a safe place from too much handling and wear. Also, a hat box like this would be a great addition to a bedroom table.

Battersea boxes, small china and porcelain boxes, have long been collector's items with the English. They come in all different shapes and most are under three inches in size. Very small objects like this are sometimes difficult to mix with the larger objects. There are several ways to make this work. All collections make more of an impact when placed together. To put one small porcelain animal or small box in each cubbyhole of a secretary makes a good display. On a table, you may want to group them together in two long lines two inches apart or in some geometric pattern. You also can put them all on a tray together and then on the table. You will find that a simple tray will not compete with the shape, color, and design of the small boxes.

All boxes are interesting and add pattern, shape, and color, and, most of all, give you a chance to choose and show your personal style.

Paperweights are fascinating accessories. The glass ones have the most intricate designs and more patterns than you could possibly imagine. These elegant and interesting accessories can be used alone on a desk or a table top or in a group.

Bowls are the most useful and varied of accessories. Here you need to stop and think. Use the trial-and-error method until you see what suits your spot and your need for color, scale, and design. Nothing is more cheerful than a bowl of well-washed, well-polished red apples on a table, particularly in winter when you are having a warming fire. The same is true of a bowl of yellow lemons to cool your room in summer. Pine cones and red berries are wonderful at Christmas. Seashells have interesting colors and shapes. They look splendid in an ocean-blue pottery bowl if this is a good color for your room. If you failed to bring some home when you last walked the beach, go to your nearest shop with aquarium supplies. The aquarium in your city will most likely have a gift shop where you can buy shells. A taller, candy-type glass jar with a top can be filled with seashells and can bring height to a table top, perhaps to balance a lamp at the opposite end of the table. Potpourri filling a small or large bowl is a great addition to a room to give it that nice fresh smell. If you put this in a bowl of good quality or value, please remember to protect the bowl with plastic or foil to keep the oil or alcohol holding the sent from discoloring the surface of your bowl.

A small framed painting held in place on a wooden plate stand or a book stand looks great on a table. A size that would be lost hanging on a wall can make a real statement. This picture will be more enjoyable and seen in greater detail if it can catch some of the light from the lamp nearby.

A big brass oval measure which once belonged to a set of scales is a wonderfully different shape to be filled with glass balls. These balls can be clear glass or colored, small as a tennis ball or large as a cantaloupe, and are plentiful around bait shops because they are used to hold up the fishermen's nets. The shells mentioned above would be beautiful in this container too. Incidentally, because the oval measure is symmetrical, it would be a great center-piece for your dining room table when you are not using fresh flowers.

Candlesticks, all sizes and kinds—from votive candles to simple sticks to candelabra—add great warmth to any room. They also can be used as a single stick, a pair, or a group made of friendly material such as all glass, wood, brass, pottery, or silver. There is no limit to the kind of room which welcomes candles. Candlelight is soft, romantic, flattering, and delightful. I recommend the use of glass or plastic bobhèches. They are inoffensive to look at and in all instances helpful in keeping the wax from dripping on the candlestick and then onto your table.

As Robert Louis Stevenson wrote, "The world is so full of a number of things, I'm sure we should all be as happy as Kings." Any object which seems attractive and appealing to you, of suitable scale for its location, can be used as an accessory to enhance the beauty, charm, and interest of your room. It will be individual and completely yours. It will show your taste and interest. Remember, good taste is its suitability. It need not have a use—a piece of sculpture is its own reason for being—but it must speak to you as something with which you want to live. The chances are very good that if it pleases you in color, texture, charm, and interest, it will do the same for your family and friends. A single blossom on your coffee table will say that someone lives here on a daily basis and that someone cares enough about himself as well as his friends and family to add a flower to brighten, cheer, and say, "This room is alive, lived in, and it welcomes you to come in and enjoy its comfort and beauty." It will be balanced, harmonious, quiet, peaceful, and all those adjectives that you have selected as your aim. Accessories are the trimming and are a golden opportunity for you to show your creativity, ingenuity, and your particular idea and ideal of beauty and charm.

Now, let's put a table together as a "how-to" example. In your living room, I know of nothing that gives the room more warmth and comfort than a rather large-sized table, square, round, oval, or rectangular, at least three by five feet in size. This table can be of almost any style or period. It can have four or six legs or a single pedestal. It can have drop leaves or a solid top. The table can be painted or of dark or light wood, and it should be of normal table height—twenty-seven to thirty inches from the floor. Put a chair on either side and a table lamp of good proportion (no more than twenty-four to twenty-six inches tall) near one chair. On the opposite end, place some kind of green plant with at least twelve inches of height above the table. In the center of the table and toward the back, place a row of your best books (leather-bound if you have them) or part of a set, maybe with red or green bindings. Use at least eight books toward the middle of the table. In front of the books, set a beautiful tea caddy, a wooden writing lap desk, or any wooden box you like. Go to your china cabinet or storage closet and get the prettiest china bowl you own, perhaps eight or ten inches across or larger, and fill it with fresh potpourri, sea shells, or beautiful polished rocks. You may want to put a small to medium-sized ashtray near the box in case anyone dares to smoke. Your table should look pretty, uncluttered, warm, and welcoming. If there is room and you have a wonderful chair height (seventeen-inch) stool, push it under the table, leaving about six inches extending out into the room. Someone will sit on it or will pull it over to the front of one of the chairs and put his feet on it. If you feel there is too little on the table top, arrange a few current magazines or a stack of three or four coffee table-sized books with the print of the spine toward the room.

Some other suggestions for your table top: If you have a collection, you may wish to feature it. If the scale is right, six or eight small boxes are interesting, and put them close together like soldiers marching toward the front. Perhaps you have a small collection of paperweights that could be used in the same formation. Never scatter your collection. Your treasures have much more impact and importance when they are placed near each other. If your collection is miniature or small animals, make them more distinct by putting them on a suitable-sized tray. Trays are wonderful for fencing in a group of things.

When you are restless and feel the need for change, try different accessories on your table. Remember scale. The things you put on a fairly big table need to be of pretty good proportions or the table will look underfurnished and the room will appear cold instead of welcoming. Let it be known that you like your room and that you do care how visitors feel in your home.

Pillows

Pillows are, of course, for comfort and for giving a feeling of coziness to a stiff, cold, and unwelcoming room.

Also, pillows provide a wonderful opportunity to experiment with a color that you want to try but are not sure how much a room can stand. If you have a solid or small, all-over pattern on your sofa, you may want to consider two fairly large pillows (twenty-two to twenty-four inches, downfilled if possible), loosely stuffed (not firm) and covered in a large, strong floral design. You may also use a solid or a contrasting color. Fringe and tassels, harking back to the Victorian era, are enjoying renewed popularity today. I think our interest in English countryside decorating has increased our appreciation for pillows to soften hard economic and political realities. You may see small needlepoint pillows in second-hand shops and resale shops. They were very popular in the 1930s and 1940s.

In the chapter on stools, I mentioned mounting needlepoint designs on a large pillow, using the fabric on the pillow like a picture mat. Cover the stitching on the outside of the needlepoint with braid or fringe. If the background of the needlepoint is black, use a black and white striped chintz or black and white mattress ticking to cover the pillow. This technique works especially well with other colors, picking up the background of the needlepoint, the striped ticking, or the chintz for the pillow.

Floor pillows are popular with children and young people for sitting around a fireplace or watching television. When not in use these are attractive stacked beside the fireplace. Inexpensive import shops always have a great selection of floor pillows in many fabrics. They are good accents both in solid colors and in patterns.

The bed in your bedroom is the perfect place for as many beautiful pillows as you wish. Delicate lacy pillows, white damask, big continental square pillows (twenty-six inches) give a matchless quality of luxury.

Small, rectangular pillows to fit your back are wonderful in wing chairs. Here I like to pick up a print fabric used elsewhere in the room. This pillow is ideal for a fringe. It should be the width of the back between the arms, and about eight to ten inches tall.

Pillows have a psychologically comforting effect. They tend to make you feel welcome. You look forward to choosing a seat in a room. Pillows are a wonderful opportunity for personal taste to shine. You may want to revive the habit of summer slip covers for your pillows, if not for your furniture. A cool, crisp, light or white cover with less trim may make your room feel airy and welcome summer.

Rest your head, your arm, and/or your back and make yourself at home.

Flowers

Flowers in the house are high on my list of priorities, even if they are only three buds of almost anything in a small give-away airline whiskey bottle to put on your bathroom counter or on your kitchen window over the sink or on your lunch tray. Your arrangements do not need to be large or important. Whatever you collect or wish to collect may turn out to be wonderful flower containers. I want to give you some ideas which are quick and effective in case flower arranging is not your best talent.

Because it is almost impossible not to be able to put one flower stem in one vase or bottle, I like to use this idea as a dining table arrangement. It is also fun to collect a certain kind of container. One idea is antique ink bottles which are inexpensive and fun to collect. Five or six in a circle either on a flat tray or on a plain glass cake stand in the center of your table make a good show. Yellow pansies look great in these because the ink bottles are usually of blue glass. Camellias, one flat blossom lying facing the ceiling in each bottle, look smashing. A second idea would be

to collect small blue and white vases (antique, fine orientals or reproductions) in a group. I believe you will find these are a pleasing way to make a centerpiece and fun to collect.

A third idea is small airline bottles in different sizes and shapes. A fourth possibility would be to plant small African violets in egg cups or demitasse cups arranged in a circle around a potted green plant in an interesting container. The same arrangement could also be done using antique shaving mugs, small pitchers, christening cups (usually silver ones with no handles), or silver mint julep cups. Anything you collect in this general size range creates a good-looking table and promotes interesting conversation.

A fifth suggestion for single-stem arrangements would be in a collection of nicely shaped individual Mateus wine bottles. They are a great shade of green. Clear glass flasks from a chemistry shop are another versatile and decorative choice. Commemorative bottles of different colors can make an interesting grouping with a flower such as a Gerber daisy in each one. Commemorative bottles are always sold in museum shops and they are attractive and easy to use. They are of a large scale, and three with perhaps three flowers in each make a pleasing arrangement on the dining or coffee table, on a desk or a secretary, or on the end of a large table. All of these are particularly suitable for the dining table because they do not block your vision.

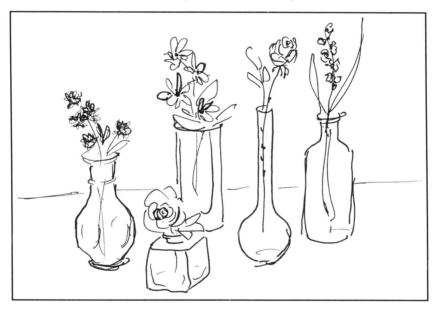

When you are shopping, keep on the lookout for pitchers, pottery and/or china, in odd shapes and colors. For an informal arrangement group three or more pitchers on your coffee table, sideboard, or dining table. Fill one with daisies, the others with colored zinnias, poppies, delphiniums, and larkspurs, and you have given a very pleasing, cheery lift to your room.

An easy container and foolproof arrangement is in something as simple as a ring mold. Buy several of these, (about eight or ten inches across) at a kitchen shop or hardware store. Paint the molds (with flat paint) using a color which works with your dining room. Mine is mustard yellow. Next cut and bend some chicken wire to fit the mold and push it down firmly. Before a party I usually cut some stems of ivy or any greenery I have in my garden and buy a bunch of colored carnations or daisies, cut the stems about one inch, and place them in the mold lying flat facing the ceiling. If you have two, three, or more of these molds down the center of your table, put a clear glass hurricane globe in the center hole with an eight- to ten-inch candle in your best low candlestick and you have an effective welcoming sight. If you are having a party using individual tables, these are charming centerpieces, particularly outside. They hold up well in the wind.

I want to make a suggestion for you when you buy one or two flats of flowers in the spring or fall to put in your garden. Plan a party at the time you are going to buy these flowers. Leave the blooming plants in their green plastic pots and put as many as possible in a large pottery or antique porcelain bowl. Impatiens, zinnias, or begonias in small pots make a breathtaking centerpiece. If your container is fragile or fine, be sure to protect it with foil or plastic. Even a non-flower arranger can create magic with blooming plants, first in the house, and then in the garden.

Simple containers such as glass cylinders or pitchers allow you to take the paper and rubber band off a bunch of flowers you have bought and put them straight down in the water where they can arrange themselves. Also, a plain pottery or oval foot-tub can be filled with a mass of flowers—one variety, no greenery showing—and placed in the center of a round wicker table on a sunporch.

One thing I do every year which gives me great pleasure is to plant paper white narcissus bulbs in water in a tall glass container. My favorite container is an antique battery jar. In case you never met a battery jar, it is a heavy glass jar used long ago in commercial garages to hold distilled

water for automobile batteries. When the spring bulbs come into the nurseries in early December I buy a dozen paper white narcissus bulbs. I put about three inches of clear marbles, rocks, or colored small rocks used in aquariums in the bottom of the containers. Then I place each bud firmly among the rocks as close together as possible and add water to cover about two-thirds of the bulbs. The rocks hold the bulbs straight, and if they grow tall, the sides of the vase or the battery jar, which should be from fourteen to sixteen inches, keep the greenery from falling over. In two or three weeks they are a mass of bloom and the pattern which the roots make in the clear water adds another dimension to this arrangement. Be sure the narcissus are placed on a table by a window where they will receive plenty of natural light and keep the water level the same. If you like, you can plant one jar each week for several weeks and keep the blooms coming. You will be delighted by the fragrance that fills the room. Once the blossoms have faded, you need not try to keep the bulbs for another season. It does not work.

People do not use bud vases much anymore, but they are lovely grouped in a cluster on your coffee table with several flowers in each. Keep them highly polished and filled with whatever is available from your garden—or buy three tulips or Gerber daisies when you are getting your groceries. This is a simple way of using something you have been storing unused and out of sight—something of your heritage, your very own, different from anyone else's.

Most everyone has a cake stand from the past tucked away in a closet. Sometimes they are glass—sometimes made of china or porcelain. When not in use for a cake, use it for a decoration—as a dining room centerpiece, on your coffee table, or for a fresh look in your entrance hall. Use six, eight, or ten polished red or green apples, oranges, or lemons to make a two-tiered stack. If you have saved an orchid, gardenia, or camellia holder as they come from the florist (green plastic with a rubber cap and a hole for the flower stem), take a single flower—a daisy, zinnia, sunflower, or a small bouquet of some violet or ivy leaves with a pansy or a few violets nestled in the center, one Carolina jasmine blossom, or a small bloom from a climbing rose—and tuck the holder filled with your bouquet in between the fruit. A charming effect. Even better if your flower has a sweet fragrance.

If you are blessed with roses, look for a rose bowl—a round, fat, small (six to eight inches across) bowl in the shape of a ball with a small (two-inch) hole in the center of the top. Many people love to arrange roses this way. Cut the stems about four to six inches long. Strip all greenery from the stems and make a round of rose blossoms (as many as possible) for a lovely, low arrangement.

Treat yourself to a few flowers, simply arranged, and place them near the chair where you most often sit. They will remind you that even in the darkness of winter, when nature seems to be asleep, spring is on its way.

Etcetera

For a bathroom that has a wash basin under the window, try this solution which covers the window and provides the missing mirror. Get a pair of shutters which fit the window. Paint the back or outside a suitable color and add a solid mirror to the inside. This gives the ability to control daylight and the convenience of a mirror.

If you have an unfortunate view out of any window in your house, perhaps this idea will improve your situation:

If there is a fence of wire, plant ivy to cover it. If your fence is of wood, begin a collection of small, interesting bird houses and attach them to the fence. They have architectural design, and who knows, you may attract a bird family to make its home there.

We often are forced to put a washer/dryer in a location that is more prominent than we like. For a way to cover this appliance, find a pair of old shutters, louvered or solid. Paint them a color suitable to the location. I hope you find this a pleasant way to screen the washer/dryer and give life to a much used spot.

Are you tired of the drooping ivy in your cache pot? Lift your spirits with a plant in a stylized shape—a topiary tree. There are many different shapes: poodle, cone, ball, etc. You may find it gives the room a new look.

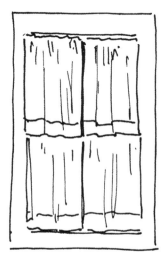

I found the need to quickly darken the windows in a child's room in a vacation house. This worked out: Buy two pairs of dark green pillowcases and two "spring rods." Rip open approximately two inches of the side seam at the back corner of each pillowcase and insert the rod through the openings. Use one pair for each rod. Hang cafe-like curtains. The decorative border of the pillow case is at the bottom of each panel.

When building bookcases on either side of a door or a pair of doors, build a shelf over the door to connect the side shelves. It gives a finished look and adds interest to the end of a room. Remember that a shelf of more than thirty inches begins to sag if it has no support and is full of books. Pull the spines of the books to the front of the shelf.

Do you have a small window in your house which you can treat like a shadow box? Try installing a pair of shutters and painting them a dark green or give them a light blue wash. Leave the shutters open. On the sill (if not wide enough add a four-inch shelf), put a country pitcher filled with wild-flowers or green grasses, a small print or a painted box of an interesting shape.

If you have a tall bookcase or a secretary in your room which needs more height, get a bird cage and place it in the center of the top. Bird cages come in all shapes, sizes, and prices. Choose one suitable for your location, and do not put anything in it. The design will add the interest.

You may have a space where a bed fits but with no room for a bedside table. I find it acceptable, workable and space saving to put a child's chair beside the bed to hold a clock and a glass. Above this, hang a pin-up or swing arm lamp. This is particularly useful in a vacation house where you often put an extra bed in a small space.

An antique child's desk with a slant top makes an interesting and suitable stand for a large dictionary. It is helpful if there is a raised strip across the bottom of the slant top to hold the dictionary in place. The antique desks are usually of walnut and do not have the ink bottle hole on the flat top.

There can never be too many books in any room. I think some extra ones stacked in a good-looking antique child's chair look inviting and attractive beside a reading chair in the living room or in the bedroom.

Some years ago small needle-point pillows were very much in fashion. Recently pillows have been growing. A way to use the small needlepoint is to mount the piece on a large pillow. I like a black and white stripe or ticking fabric to frame the often used black background. Use some braid to cover the attaching stitches.

Do you need an extra table to use as a coffee table or beside a chair? Go to the Army-Navy store and buy a folding camp stool. Find a large tray in your storage closet and put it on the folding stool for a useful, handsome table.

If you have inherited a pier glass mirror and there is no wall on which to hang it, do consider hanging it over a sofa, even if it goes from ceiling mold to the back of the sofa. It works!

Occasionally you will find yourself wanting to use the space in front of a never-opened door. Instead of removing the door, paint it the same color as the wall, pretend it is a wall, and place your furniture arrangement as if it were not there. When you hang a picture, center it as you would if it were a continuous wall.

Decorating Rules

Some time ago, *House Beautiful* published an article which included Ten Golden Rules of Decorating, put together by a group of decorators. I think the rules are excellent, so I am taking the liberty of including them in this book. There are many good things about rules because, if followed, the end result will have a quality we all seek—harmony. This comes principally from the fundamentals of good design. I feel their Ten Golden Rules are certainly worth listing, but remember that rules, once learned, are also meant to be broken, or at least bent.

I. **Classic**—An orderly balance chiefly created by the return to geometric shapes: rectangles, squares, circles, etc.

II. **Comfort**—In the introduction to this book, extensively I described the meaning of comfort to me. This is different for everyone, but creature comforts are places in your home to eat, read, nap, and daydream. "Some people confuse luxury with grandeur. To me, comfort is perhaps the ultimate luxury." (Billy Baldwin) Comfort prevails in rooms which pamper the senses.

III. "The desire for **symmetry,** for **balance,** and for **rhythm** is one of the most inveterate of human instincts." (Edith Wharton and Ogden Goodman, Jr.)

IV. **Suitability**—Elsie de Wolfe said, "We must learn to recognize suitability, simplicity and proportion, and apply our knowledge to our needs." You are the one who will best know what is suitable for your way of life, your taste, and your budget. The Shakers and their furniture perhaps best demonstrate suitability for the strict law-abiding followers of their faith. They insisted on order, cleanliness, and utility without ostentation. Elsie de Wolfe is really the head of the decorating family today, certainly of those whose watch words are comfort, suitability, simplicity, and proportion. She was the person who brought light and air into the world of heavy draperies and layers of curtains where one would have sufficed. She was especially sensitive in her decorating to the suitability of fabric to the surroundings, the furniture, and the people who live in the room. Elsie de Wolfe had great respect for the client.

V. **Color**—"There should never be any doubt about what your color has to say. It may be lemon yellow, watermelon pink, chocolate brown or anything you like, just as long as it knows its own mind." (Dorothy Draper) In this book, the chapter on color will help you find your place in the rainbow.

VI. **Passion**—As Michael Greer said, "You need one marvelous decorative object which you love outrageously, which you may have spent far more for than you could afford. It can be anything, a painting or a rug or a vase, as well as a piece of furniture. This item will be the focal point and excitement of the room."

VII. **Warmth**—David Hicks states, "I may create a very disciplined background, but I like things messed up or cozied up a little. I am always thinking of warmth." Objects such as fat pillows, a throw over the back of a chair, good lighting, or books are some of the things that add warmth.

VIII. **Contrast**—"If a room is too rich, or if the furniture is all too ornate or all too primitive, the room is wrong. It is contrast that brings it excitingly alive." (Michael Taylor) A stool is a great piece of furniture to use as contrast, or a classical lamp on a country table.

IX. **Scale**—"Build in such a manner, and with such proportions, that all the parts together may convey a sweet harmony to the eyes of the beholder." (Andrea Palladia) Human scale comfort is always a consideration.

X. **Personal style**—"Why do we love certain houses, and why do they seem to love us? It is the warmth of our individual hearts reflected in our surroundings." (T. H. Robsjohn Gibbons) Personal treasures collected over the years, often something brought from your childhood home, often something brought from your travels, but always something close to your heart, reflect your personal style. Remember what Sister Parish said: "Don't go shopping; use what you have."

Decorating your home is, above all, an exciting opportunity for you to say, "This is the kind of place in which I choose to live." It is an opportunity for you to think about what makes you comfortable, about how you feel when you are surrounded by your favorite things. Does that first daffodil in a simple bottle on your coffee table lift your spirits and say to you "Spring is on the way"? Notice if your room seems to say, "Why did you plan to go out today? You will really enjoy and feel renewed by the pleasure of staying in this comfortable room with its warmth and charm." If this thought crosses your mind, chances are quite good that you have made your room a place which is right for you. This feeling is what decorating is about.

Vacation Home

Simple, easy living, easy to care for, easy to open, easy to close. These are things I look for and think about in a vacation house. Windows that open and shut easily with

good screens. There always seem to be bugs and extra animals around these second homes. Comfort, as well as a
pleasant look, is the name of the game. Do not make this
a final resting place for your old, almost worn-out mat-
tresses. Rest is one thing you came for, so be sure you can
get a good night's sleep. This home is mainly for you, so

comfortable chairs are in order, as always. Good reading lamps and nice generous tables are essential, too. In the living room, add at least one big table for puzzles, playing solitaire, writing, thinking, eating, and admiring the view. People do gravitate to big tables. A partial or empty table is a really appealing space and a welcoming entrance.

Retirement Home

Change is not always easy. When you face moving from your present home to a retirement home, it is one of the most emotionally jarring experiences of your life. The decision is usually due to some change in life's circumstances, such as age, widowhood, poor health, financial considerations, or a combination. Each of these is a saddening, upsetting experience. On the other hand, the move may turn out to be a pleasant relief from the burden and responsibility of your present way of life.

To begin with, your space will be smaller than where you are now living. More than likely it will be the size of your very first home, which, if you will remember, you were very excited and thrilled about. You also used all the creative imagination you could muster to make it particularly warm, cozy, and suitable for your way of life. So take these qualities with you as you move to the place in which you expect to spend the rest of your life.

The requisite necessities are indeed the same: your comfortable bed, your own chair and ottoman, and the largest table your space will allow to go beside it. This will hold your good reading lamp, your basket or tray of sewing, mail, reading material, and one thing which comes from nature (a flower, a plant, or a bowl of fruit). Near this table you should pull up a chair, such as a dining room armchair. You may want to use this when writing or playing solitaire. I hope this table or your comfortable chair can be placed at a window where you can enjoy looking outside. You should provide, if space permits, comfortable seating for two or three visitors.

Storage of your personal possessions will be the next question to be addressed. Your personal wardrobe perhaps will need to be seriously reduced because closet space will not be equal to that to which you have been accustomed. You will, of course, keep what you will use and enjoy and probably keep one frivolous garment for old time's sake. Your bed and table linens will also need to be pared down and will be stored in the large drawer of your chest with extra bed covers, or on your closet shelves. It may work out better if you have a chest near your dining table which can be devoted to flat silver, table, and/or bed linens.

Now, let us decide about taking the things you cannot live without. I am not speaking of a telephone, radio, or television. I am speaking of something you treasure from your childhood home, something belonging to someone, now departed, with whom you shared some part of your life. You alone are able to decide what these items are, but I urge you to not let them go. They are your things. Among these things which are part of you and your life are photographs and books. Photographs can be reframed and hung on walls or unframed and put in albums to still enjoy and save space. You can always have a storage box under your bed filled with things not to be parted with, but to be tagged for certain children, young people, or friends to be given at suitable times.

There will be a collection of things that, if you put on your thinking cap, can be offered and where they can find a suitable and pleasure-giving resting place. I will give a few examples; perhaps some of these will fit your treasure: The dress you wore to graduation, to make your debut, or to be presented to the queen should be offered to a heritage society, a small museum, library, small private school, or to a clothes museum. They may welcome it. You will know that if they accept it, it will be well protected, displayed, and cared for always. If you have an interesting collection, try to label each piece as your best knowledge lets you and see if it can be used as a teaching tool. If you cannot locate a protected resting place for your collection, contact a respectable antique dealer or an estate sale person and see if they can help you find a buyer. You may want to have these items photographed and later write a story about these for your grandchildren.

You may need or want to sell your "Sunday Best" possessions for which you will not have room in your new home. If you do not need the money, consider giving a suitable painting, a piece of furniture or silver to each member of your family. If this does not suit you, call in a professional to put a price on each of these things. If it is to be an estate sale and circumstances make it wiser for you to sell, ask family to come first, then close friends, and the rest turn over to the estate sale person to dispose of. Please don't do any giving or selling until you have moved. Only then can you be sure whether you have room for one more piece of furniture or painting to go to your new home. It may make you feel happy that the possessions which have decorated your life and have given you and your family and friends so much joy and beauty will add quality or charm to the lives of the new owners and make their lives more pleasant.

A few last words: If your new smaller place is painted

hospital green and really dampens your spirits, you can get permission to repaint even if you are not an owner. Select a color which will be light, cheerful, and pleasant to you. See how much charm you can get in this new small space. Maybe your furniture will be used in different and interesting ways. Your desk perhaps could double as a bedside table. Remember from the beginning of this book I have admitted having a love affair with big flat surfaces—tables to be specific. Try to keep one available for a jigsaw puzzle which you have never had time for before, a big dictionary for word games, and always a deck of cards, Monopoly, dominoes, or a new hobby.

I believe you will find that this new space can be a real challenge, and you can make it a comfortable, warm, inviting, and charming home. Maybe you will inspire your new neighbor when he or she comes to call. Keep a tea pot and cookies handy!

Note to the Reader

My hope is that by the time you finish this book you will have fallen in love either for the first time or once again with the space allotted to you, your home. I hope you see your home as a many faceted space which is yours, a space in which you can create, change, and recreate the way in which you live. Always remember that comfort and warmth add an important and necessary part to your life. This is "your place" in which to retreat from the bustle of the outside world. As the young people of the 1960s often left home to "find themselves and who they were," I believe that you, the reader, can learn who you are by defining your space and creating your home.

"We shape our dwellings and afterwards our dwellings shape us."—**Winston Churchill**